D1150930

READY
TO
GROW

READY
TO
GROW

PRACTICAL STEPS TO
KNOWING GOD BETTER

ALLAN HARKNESS

Scripture Union books are published in Australia by
Scripture Union Australia
Resources for Ministry Unit
PO Box 77
Lidcombe
NSW 1825,
Australia

and in the United Kingdom by
Scripture Union
207–209 Queensway
Bletchley, MK2 2EB
England

Harkness, Allan.
Ready to grow: practical steps to knowing God better.

Bibliography.
ISBN   0 949720 71 2.

1. God – Knowableness. 2. God – Biblical teaching. I.
Scripture Union. II. Title.

231.042

All Scripture passages are taken from *The Bible for Today – Contemporary
English Version* published by © American Bible Society, 1991, 1995
unless indicated otherwise.

Drawings by Helen Kelly
Design by Kelvin Young, Preston
Printed by Australian Print Group, Maryborough

CONTENTS

AN OPEN LETTER TO CHURCH LEADERS

Dear Christian colleague,

I know that one of your greatest desires as a church leader is to see your people learning to listen to God and to respond to him in loving obedience.

A key means by which they can do this is through a regular encounter with God – and Bible reading and prayer are central components of this encounter. Such relationship-building is as essential for spiritual growth as corporate worship and study groups.

This handbook outlines practical ways for Christians to develop their skills in this area. But, with so many pressures facing them today, they will need your active support to persevere. Will you help?

* Pray that enthusiasm for regular time with God, in Bible reading and prayer, will be caught by people in your church, and that their response will be of God's Holy Spirit.

* Actively demonstrate the centrality of the Bible for Christian growth in all facets of your church life. For example, integrate this with church worship (see Chapter 7).

❋ Teaching of skills is as important as motivating. Ensure ways are provided for people to develop appropriate skills.

❋ Small groups (such as home cells, Bible study groups) are especially good situations for encouraging people to develop their devotional life (see Chapter 7).

❋ Point people to useful resources. For example, Scripture Union's Bible reading resources for people of all ages. (An SU Bible reading representative in your church can play a key part in promoting these. Contact your local SU office for details of how to appoint one.)

❋ Special promotional thrusts are valuable – but work best when part of ongoing 'drip-feed' encouragement over an extended period.

My experience shows that the effectiveness of your ministry will be enhanced as you foster Christian growth in this way – and better enable your church to accomplish the mission to which it has been called!

In the Kingdom's ventures,

Allan Harkness

INTRODUCTION
to the original edition

*'How blessed is anyone
who ... delights in the
law of Yahweh and
murmurs his law day
and night. Such a one is
like a tree planted near
streams; it bears fruit in
season ...'*

PSALM 1:1-3
(JERUSALEM BIBLE)

I'm fascinated by trees – from the huge Kauris and delicate Kowhais I've seen when walking in the New Zealand mountains; apple and pear trees as I've picked the luscious fruit for overseas markets; to the beautiful parks in Singapore, where I stroll among numerous palms and trees with incredible surface root systems.

Have you ever given a tree your whole attention? Have you wondered how it survives, especially in the heat of summer? The earth is hard and dry; the grass is withered and brown; there's not a drop of water to be seen. Yet the tree stands tall, strong, green and alive – for deep below the surface there is life-giving water for its roots to absorb. The tree grows almost miraculously – because of the hidden sources of nourishment.

This is the theme of the first Psalm in the Bible, and the reason I wanted to write this handbook. Most Christians want to know the secrets of survival – none of us want to fail when we are under pressure, or lose our faith and confidence in God when things get tough.

What are the secrets of Christian growth?

The writer in Psalm 1 describes a tree with green leaves and plentiful fruit. Its secret is in the stream nearby. The writer also describes people who remain alive and growing, even when the dry winds blow. The secret for these people is their habit of seeking nourishment from God's message to us. And this is the purpose of this book. It aims to help ordinary followers of Jesus develop the most important aspect of their lives – a regular encounter with the living God in the Bible and prayer. So – if you are ready to grow, this handbook is for you!

You won't find in these pages a recipe for instant 'success' as a Christian – or learn how to become a 'heavyweight' overnight: only as God's Holy Spirit works within us do we become more and more like

Jesus. The techniques outlined are of little value in themselves but they represent a valuable discipline which can help you get started and keep going – and growing!

Chapter 1 discusses the value of setting time aside specifically to focus on God. Chapter 2 sets out the essential elements of this time, and outlines a four-step method to get you started – and each of these steps is developed in detail in Chapters 3–6. Chapter 7 recognises a variety of situations with other people in which spiritual growth can be encouraged. Chapter 8 outlines a variety of creative methods to incorporate into your time with God: try those that appeal to you.

Experiment with the ideas in this handbook. Modify them to suit your situation, and let these suggestions spark other possibilities. Flexibility and creativity are the key! Appendix 2 describes further resource books which can help you to get to grips with the Bible and Appendix 3 provides the titles of more general books on topics related to the theme of this book.

Most of the contents of this book have existed in one form or another for many years. I have been introduced to these principles particularly through my contact with Scripture Union and various people in that movement have been instrumental in my own spiritual growth. If this book whets your appetite for deepening your friendship with God, it will have been worth writing.

With Paul,

I pray that your love will keep on growing and that you will
fully know and understand how to make the right choices.
Then you will still be pure and innocent when Christ returns.
And until that day, Jesus Christ will keep you busy doing good
deeds that bring glory and praise to God (Philippians 1:9-11).

A NOTE
on the second edition

In the years since the first edition of *Ready to Grow* was
published, our world has undergone incredible
changes – in national and international politics,
environmental concerns, economics, technology.

Similar changes can be readily identified also in the
ways people think and perceive the world around them.
Some call it 'postmodernity', others the 'Generation X
syndrome'. Whatever you might call these changes,
they are making an immense impact on all aspects of
our lives. And how people understand spirituality and
spiritual development has not been immune from these
changes. No longer can we assume that the traditional
expressions of the disciplines of the Christian life will
continue to be observed by Christians, either as
individuals or when we meet with others.

This revision of *Ready to Grow* incorporates insights
that take this changing outlook into account. It seeks

to recognise and conserve the best of past practices while recognising that today's people may express important spiritual principles differently to those of older generations. However, the goal remains the same – to provide people who are seeking to develop their relationship with God with relevant resources and skills to do this more effectively in their own unique situations. As they mature in their faith, they will then be better able to actively participate in the mission of God's people, the Church.

To that end I re-offer this handbook to the people of God's special community, his Church.

Grapes

GROWING A
RELATIONSHIP
WITH GOD

'The true purpose of
our existence in this
world is, quite
simply, to look for
God, and in looking,
to find him, and
having found Him,
to love Him...'

MALCOLM
MUGGERIDGE

Humans seem to have three basic built-in aspirations:

* to understand what is 'really real' beyond physical and material experience,
* to have a sense of significance and,
* to be accepted as part of a community.

The quest for these things is what spirituality is about, and people seek to develop their spirituality in diverse ways.

The heart of the Good News brought by Jesus Christ finds that these aspirations are met most fully in a relationship with the living God. The basis of being a Christian is not what you know or do but *who* you know who will help meet your deepest needs. Jesus himself said, 'Eternal life is to know you, the only true God, and to know Jesus Christ, the one you sent' (John 17:3).

We live in the information age. Sophisticated communication technology is commonplace with easy access to the internet and e-mail, mobile phones and satellite TV making the world seem very close – and very small. However, greater still than these forms of contact is that we can *know* the God of history, the creator of life, and become his friend – and come as close to him as a child to its loving parent. Jesus made this possible for us when he died on the cross 2000 years ago.

Christian spirituality is all about nurturing this friendship with God and has two main parts. On one 'side of the coin' is a growing desire to actively build stronger relationship links through the 'disciplines' of Christian living, especially understanding and applying the Bible, and prayer. On the other 'side of the coin' is a life of loving, obedient action that demonstrates the strengthening of these links.

However, spirituality does not just 'happen' nor friendships continue or deepen without communication. We need to allow time to meet God so as to deepen our relationship with him. This is a two-way process as we open ourselves to God and he responds to us. The writer of this Psalm knew this:

Each morning you listen to my prayer,
as I bring my requests to you
and wait for your reply (Psalm 5:3).

SPECIAL TIME WITH GOD

Generations of Christians have valued the principle of setting aside a specific time to be with God, making it part of their daily lives. They recognise that God is present with them through the various situations and activities of each day, and also that it is important to meet with other Christians (see Chapter 7). And, they also realise that meeting by themselves with God is a vital ingredient in their spiritual growth. The Bible records the names of many people who have followed

17

this principle, including Daniel (Daniel 6:10), David (Psalm 55:17), Peter (Acts 10:9), Paul (2 Timothy 1:3) and Jesus himself (Mark 1:35).

Various names have been given to this special relationship-building time, but they all mean the same thing: an appointment with God, when a Christian meets with him through purposeful Bible reading and prayer. The purpose of spending time with God is not to earn heavenly credit points, nor to do 'the right religious thing'. It is not meant to be a dry religious ritual but rather a way of life that provides us with the opportunity to acknowledge who God is. We celebrate his life in us, and get our lives into perspective as we discover his purposes. In this time we offer God our *devotion*, our loyalty and obedient, faithful service – so this time is commonly described as 'daily devotions'.

FINDING TIME IN A BUSY LIFE

Spending time with God is as basic to Christian living as food and water are to our physical survival. The very busyness of our lives is reason enough to plan a regular encounter with God, allowing him to speak to us in the midst of the various pressures and concerns we face. By immersing ourselves in God's concerns we see our own in perspective, and this keeps us from becoming overwhelmed by them.

This book presents different ideas to help busy people

develop their own special time with God. To benefit from these ideas, you may need to modify your daily routine. 'Discipline' is not a popular concept today, so if you have trouble setting aside time to spend with God in this way, perhaps you need to examine your priorities. Ask yourself 'How much do I *really* want a living relationship with God? What priority am I willing to give to this?'

Silver Wattle

GETTING
STARTED

'Listen to the wind Nicodemus! Now, Nicodemus, the Spirit of God is just like that – invisible yet unmistakable, impalpable yet full of power, able to do wonderful things for you if only you will stand in its path and turn your face to it and open your life to its influence.'

JAMES STEWART

INGREDIENTS FOR YOUR SPECIAL MEETING WITH GOD

What are the key ingredients of this special time for meeting with God?

An open attitude

Remember you are meeting God, who knows what is best for you – even though sometimes you might not understand where he is taking you. Be open to what God wants to say to you, and how you can respond. It may mean surprises or require radical changes in your life.

A time

Most of us are 'creatures of habit' and regular habits can be useful. If you plan to meet God at the same time and in the same place each day, this can help you to come prepared.

Choose a time when you are alert, unlikely to be interrupted and able to put to one side any pressing needs.

* Many people find first thing in the morning is ideal, as they are fresh and less likely to be pressured by other concerns and unplanned interruptions. They begin the new day with God and can trust him to take care of all that is to happen during it.

* Some people prefer the evening – but make sure you are sufficiently awake!

❋ Others prefer to take time out during the day – a
mealtime, while commuting to work by train or bus,
or a few minutes between other responsibilities.
Experiment until you find the time that suits you
best.

How long should I spend?

The *quality* of time spent with God is more important
than the quantity. You could start with five to ten
minutes. As you grow closer to God you will find you
desire to spend a longer time with him. God knows
your situation and the time you have available – so it
really depends on how much you want to grow in your
friendship with him.

A place

Find a place where you can focus on God, ideally
somewhere relatively quiet and free from distractions.
Most people focus more easily on God when alone.
However, if you cannot find such a place, you may still
be able to ignore what is happening around you and
discover spiritual, rather than physical solitude.

Don't be daunted!

Do not be daunted if at first you are unable to find the
'ideal' time and place. *Flexibility* and *creativity* are keys
to resolving such difficulties.

Negotiate with those you live with for time and space. You could ask your house-mate(s) not to chat to you for a few minutes or let the family know that the closed door in the evening means 'please do not disturb'. However, make sure you don't create misunderstandings as you work out these practical details.

Be creative in making time to spend alone with God. All of us face pressures – but whether you are an office worker, a business person who commutes for several hours each day, a member of a large family in a small home or apartment, or a busy mother with pre-school children – you can still find some time.

If, despite your efforts, you do not find a satisfactory block of time each day, develop the skill of meeting God many times during the day. Find a minute here, several there. Or plan for an extended interval once or twice a week when someone else is able to mind any pre-school children and keep them out of earshot. You might even find that an occasional formal or self-managed retreat suits your personal circumstances better.

A Bible

Choose a version of the Bible that you can readily understand. Many people appreciate the *Contemporary English Version* but there are many other versions such as the *New International Version*, the *Good News Version* and the

New Revised Standard Version. Ask a Christian friend or church leader to help you select the right version for you. A paraphrase like Eugene Petersen's *The Message*, can also be helpful.

Paper and pen

Keep some paper or a notebook handy to jot down things that come to mind, to help you to keep track of what God is telling you.

A FOUR-STEP PATTERN TO GET YOU STARTED

The following four-step pattern provides a helpful structure for these regular times with God. (See Appendix 1 for the basis of this method.)

Prepare

Consciously prepare yourself to meet with God by opening your life to his presence and expecting to receive from him.

❋ Use a simple prayer, such as 'Lord, as I meet you now please help me to listen carefully to you and to respond obediently'.

❋ Because God is the author of the Bible, ask him to help you understand what the particular Bible passage might mean for your unique situation. Perhaps you could pray Psalm 119:18 – 'Open my mind, and let me discover the wonders of your Law'.

NOTE: Chapter 3, 'Prepare to meet with God', discusses this stage in greater detail.

Read

Read an appropriate section of the Bible, taking time to 'get the feel' of what is written. Sometimes you will need to read the section through several times.

The Gospels in the New Testament are a good place to start. You could perhaps read through Mark's Gospel – to meet Jesus and see how he lived.

NOTE: Chapter 4, 'Read the Bible', will help you develop this step further.

Explore

Think about the meaning of the passage. Three especially helpful questions are:

* What is the main point of the passage?
* What does the passage tell me about God? *In some parts of the Bible we read only of God the Father; in others we read about Jesus (God's Son) or the Holy Spirit.*
* What might God be saying to me personally through this passage? *In what ways can I apply the Bible's principles in my own circumstances and relationships?*

Use your notebook to write down your discoveries. If using a printed resource such as one of Scripture Union's Bible reading booklets, read its comments at this point.

NOTE: Chapter 5, 'Explore – the Bible and life together', provides further insights to help you ask appropriate and relevant questions about the meaning of the Bible passage.

Respond

Respond to your discoveries.

❋ Make your insights the basis of your prayer. Praise God for who he is and what you have discovered about him. Thank him for what he is doing in your life. Apologise for your failures and ask his forgiveness. Ask him to meet your needs and those of others.

❋ Meeting God is life-changing. To make your time with God worthwhile, it needs to have an impact on your daily life. Ask God to help you live out what you have learned – at home, at work, in relationships – indeed, in the whole of your life.

❋ Christians are not meant to live in isolation. Look for opportunities to share your discoveries about God with others, in both word and action. You may be able to use these insights to encourage and help another person, such as a family member, another Christian or a friend who is not yet a Christian. NOTE: Read Chapter 6, 'Respond to God' and Chapter 7, 'Share your discoveries', to develop these ideas in greater detail.

This 4-step pattern can be varied according to your needs and how much variety you desire. Chapter 8, 'Try these methods', presents a range of creative methods which can also be used within this basic pattern.

3

Apples

PREPARE TO MEET
WITH GOD

'Naturally, when the
storm is roaring
within us we shall
never hear a pin
drop; but God, when
he comes, comes only
on the feet of doves,
and we must be
still.'

HELMUT
THIELICKE

It is important to prepare yourself for your meeting with God, for the more you put into it, the more you will receive.

While God is always with you, your perception of his presence is heightened when you set aside a special time to be with him. However busy your life, this is one part of the day that should not be hurried, or you may feel dissatisfied and cheated.

Set realistic goals for what you can achieve in the time available, so make your time with God unhurried, irrespective of whether you have five minutes or one hour.

YOUR TIME WITH GOD IN CONTEXT

As a whole and complex person be aware of your present personal situation as you meet with God in the particular context of your life:

* Are worries, fears, sins and doubts threatening to engulf you? Acknowledge these, then put them to one side for now. As you deliberately set your sights on the living God rather than yourself, you will be able to see your problems in perspective.

* Joyfully and gratefully acknowledge the positive things that are happening to you.

* Look ahead. Browse through your diary or think about coming events. Glance at the newspaper to

remind you of any community or world events that may affect your outlook for the day.

FOCUS ON GOD

Now, turn your attention on God. Consciously develop the ability to bring your whole self – not just your mind, but also your emotions, spirit and body – to focus on 'God's glory shining in the face of Christ' (2 Corinthians 4:6, *Good News Bible*). There are a number of ways you can do this:

❋ Spend time reflecting on God in silence. Think about his qualities of faithfulness, constant love, justice and mercy. Recall ways he has revealed them. This should lead you into worshipping God, recognising his 'worthship'. Tell God of your love for him, and any doubts and anxieties you have about your relationship with him.

❋ Remove distractions by closing your eyes. This should help you to focus on God. Alternatively, open your eyes to allow parts of God's creation to arouse your sense of worship. Some people find a picture, a cross or a candle helpful, even a flower or the view through a window.

❋ Read a psalm of praise or a prayer from the Bible (Try Psalms 24, 93, or 131; Nehemiah 9:5b-6; Luke 1:46-55; parts of Ephesians 1:3-14). Choose a

written prayer from a book of prayers or church
service book such as the Anglican prayer book.

❋ Use music. Listen to any piece of music that assists
you to focus on God – a meditative piece, song of
praise, hymn or something entirely different. You may
wish to sing aloud.

Posture

Make your body posture a part of this focusing process.
Some find it helpful to raise their hands to God; others
cup their hands to symbolise their openness to receiving
Christ's love.

To encourage your worship, choose a position that
helps you to relax physically. Although kneeling is
commonly mentioned in the Bible, other possibilities like
standing, sitting and even lying face down on the floor
may be more suitable for you. Sitting is more appropriate
for reading the Bible but if you plan to write, a hard
surface such as a table is better.

Experiment to find what suits you – you may like to
choose several different postures during your time with
God – sitting, standing, kneeling, even moving around
and dancing!

After focusing on God and his presence with you, ask
him to meet you through the Bible passage you are about
to read. Ask the Holy Spirit to enable you to discern what

God is saying to you through it.

DISTRACTIONS

At first, it may seem that everything conspires to distract you and you become very conscious of interruptions and wandering thoughts. These will continue, but as you mature in your relationship with God, you will learn to cope with them effectively.

Avoidable distractions

❋ Are you constantly interrupted? Explain to family members or housemates why you need this time alone. Request them to leave you undisturbed for these few minutes.

❋ To prevent telephone calls distracting you, take the handpiece off the hook and turn off your pager or mobile phone. If possible, have someone take phone messages for you.

❋ Is your location too noisy? Find a quieter place or plan to use a different time of the day. Perhaps rising before others in your household would solve this problem.

❋ Are you distracted by what is around you, such as piles of paperwork on your desk? Move elsewhere, or face another direction.

❋ Use the sounds that distract you, like birds singing,

children crying, a plane flying overhead. Let them be a
stimulus for brief prayer rather than an enemy. When
dealt with in this way distraction often disappears.

Wandering thoughts

When you find your thoughts straying from God you may
feel guilty and discouraged. Shutting them out, saying, 'I
will *not* think of these things', will merely make the
problem worse!

Allow your mind to come under the control and
lordship of Jesus Christ. You will need *discipline* to 'take
every thought captive and make it obey Christ' (2
Corinthians 10:5, *GNB*). These points may help you do
this more effectively:

* Eliminate any distracting physical factor. Tiredness is a
  common cause of a wandering mind. If your best time
  for spending with God is in the morning, remember
  that 'alertness at 6.00am stems from what you were
  doing at 10.00pm the night before'! A stuffy, poorly
  ventilated room may cause your mind to wander, so
  aim for a comfortable room temperature, as neither
  extremes of discomfort nor excessive comfort are
  helpful.
* Lapses in concentration or disinterest in your time
  with God can signal a barrier between you and God.
  You may need to deal with sin to restore your

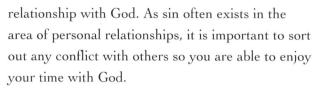

relationship with God. As sin often exists in the area of personal relationships, it is important to sort out any conflict with others so you are able to enjoy your time with God.

* When particular people come to mind, God may be prompting you to pray for them or contact them. Pray briefly for them or make a note on paper to deal with it later.

* Similarly, if you think of something that needs attention, jot it down for later.

When you find yourself daydreaming or distracted, apologise to God before moving on. Don't be afraid to talk with God about whatever is pre-occupying you, for God is interested in every detail of your life.

4

Eucalyptus Blossom

READ THE
BIBLE

'Every word of the scriptural text is a window or door leading us out of the tarpaper shacks of self into this great outdoors of God's revelation in sky and ocean, tree and flower, Isaiah and John, and, finally and completely, Jesus.'

EUGENE
PETERSON

THE BIBLE: A VERY SPECIAL BOOK

Many different voices shout for our attention – the internet and television, radio and video, advertisements, shop windows, the printed media, friends and leaders. To which should we pay attention? Which *really* matter?

As our lives become increasingly dominated by the values and concerns of a world opposed to God's ways, it is essential to listen to the voice which ultimately counts, the voice of the living God. God communicates with us in a variety of ways – in creation, through events and other people. But the primary means by which God speaks to us is through the Bible, which is why the Bible is called 'the Word of God' and 'God's Word'. The Bible is more than just a record of God's dealings with the human race; it is a key to growth for Christians. Through reading it we learn of God's character and concerns. We get to know him better, learning how to bring our ways into line with his. Paul summarises its value when he writes to Timothy:

> *Everything in the Scriptures is God's Word. All of it is useful for teaching and helping people and for correcting them and showing them how to live. The Scriptures train God's servants to do all kinds of good deeds (2 Timothy 3:16-17).*

If we are to become the people God intends us to be, we must allow our lives to be shaped by him. Through reading the Bible we become *participants* in God's plans for us and his world. Meeting God there will naturally lead us to want to respond to him in a variety of ways: first in prayer, which then flows out into obedient and loving action in the world. God has placed us there to be effective members of society, acting as 'salt' and 'light'. Salt enhances the taste of food, acting as a cleanser and preserver. In the past, it has even acted as a fertiliser. Light expels darkness, showing off beauty (see Matthew 5:13-16).

The Bible as a whole book

God has revealed himself through the whole Bible. From the accounts of creation in Genesis, through to John's 'Come, Lord Jesus!' in Revelation (22:20, *GNB*), we learn about the scope of God's character, his concern for people, and his relationships with them.

Some parts of the Bible seem far removed from our personal circumstances, but if we read only the familiar or easy parts (like just the New Testament or our favourite Psalms) we deny ourselves the chance of seeing the full picture. When we read the whole of the Bible over a period of time, its overall message becomes clearer. We gain an understanding of the larger vision, grasp the meaning of specific passages and books more easily, becoming better equipped to apply their insights to our lives.

Many Christians have found they benefited from reading the major parts of the Bible over a period of three to five years. Printed guides are available to help you do this – see Appendix 2 for suggestions.

Applying the Bible

'For some sixty years, the daily message covering in an orderly way both Old and New Testaments, and supplemented for most of that period by the expository notes, has descended like a refreshing rain upon my spirit. Day by day there has come challenge, rebuke, guidance, inspiration and sometimes questions and doubts, but the overall effect has been to condition all my thinking with the broad tenor of the God-given Word. The Bible is a book of spiritual principles, and it is a grasp of the broad sweep of these principles that is important. Key verses and specialised study are of value, but it is all too easy to lose sight of the forest as a whole, while becoming too preoccupied with some of the individual branches and twigs of trees...'[1]

John Laird

WHERE IN THE BIBLE DO I START TO READ?

Starting at the first book of the Bible and working through to the end is unlikely to be helpful. In Chapter 2 we suggested you start with a Gospel. Using that as your starting point, try the following sequence:

* Spend two or three weeks working through the first four or five chapters of Mark's Gospel. As a guide, use the section divisions found in most contemporary versions of the Bible.
* Read one of Paul's letters (e.g. Philippians).
* Move to an Old Testament historical book (e.g. Exodus chapters 1–18).
* Next, follow with a group of Psalms (e.g. 90–106).
* Return to the Gospel for a few more chapters.
* Dig into an Old Testament prophetic book (e.g. Amos or Hosea), and so on.

Read passages of the Bible consecutively. Work through the Bible books or large sections of the longer books in the order their chapters appear. This will help you appreciate the natural flow of the book, and to understand the sections in the context of their place in the book.

Build variety into your reading. Sometimes you may want to explore *themes* of the Bible, such as what God is like; the Holy Spirit; serving God; Christian character, etc. This is a worthwhile exercise so long as you are aware of one potential danger when you look only at a few verses, misunderstanding can arise as you isolate phrases and ideas from their natural context. ('See passages in their context' on page 55.) Scripture Union's *Foothold* series is a good place to start for a balance of consecutive and thematic reading.

When passages from different books of the Bible fit naturally together, link them. For example:

❋ Before reading Paul's letters to the Thessalonians, read about the visit Paul made to Thessalonica that led to his letter-writing (Acts 17:1-15).

❋ Many of the Psalms were written in response to particular situations. To appreciate the depth of David's feelings in Psalm 51, refer to 2 Samuel 11:1–12:25 to understand the event that led him to write the Psalm.

Find similar linked passages by consulting the introductions to Bible books, footnotes, and the cross-references printed in most Bibles (cross-references are verses that relate in some way to the one you are looking at).

At special times of the year, such as Easter and Christmas, you may wish to read Bible passages that are especially appropriate. For example:

❋ At *Easter* read Luke 22–24; or Matthew 26–28.

❋ At *Christmas* read Luke 2 and Matthew 1:18–2:12.

HOW MUCH SHOULD I READ EACH DAY?

Be flexible. Read as much as the natural divisions of the passage determine, allowing time to think about the passage and pray.

The books of the Bible contain a variety of types of writing, and this will affect how long a passage you should read. For example, the Gospel narratives divide easily into relatively short sections (and most modern versions indicate these by subheadings). In the historical books of the Old Testament (e.g. Genesis, 1 & 2 Kings) you may need to read a whole chapter before coming to a natural break in the story. In Proverbs, a book of wise sayings with no story line, you may manage only two or three verses at a time.

HOW SHOULD I READ?

Your regular time with God is not designed for detailed intellectual analysis of the Bible passage, but for prayerful consideration and exploration to see what God might be saying to you. This will strengthen your relationship with him. As the words hit home, allow the Holy Spirit to show you what you should do next. Then you can say you are 'listening' to God – with his Spirit meeting with your spirit, conveying to you what God wants from you as you respond to what you are hearing.

This style of reading is often called 'devotional reading'. It is important to distinguish between reading for *information* and reading for *formation.* Devotional reading is not so much concerned with acquiring knowledge as with transforming our lives and relationships.

More than one process is at work when you read devotionally so you will need to employ different methods to those normally used to process written information. Here are some practical hints to help you read effectively:

* Read slowly.
* Read the passage several times, perhaps in different Bible versions.
* Read carefully to understand what the passage is *actually* saying rather than what you think it *ought* to be saying!
* Savour the passage. Sometimes you will need to read the passage in full to feel the force of its message; at other times you might pick out a verse or a line to mull over before moving on.
* Try to imagine yourself in the situation, as a participant or spectator.

Reading the Bible this way is especially helpful for your regular times with God. These will need to be complemented with times of in-depth Bible study, when your intellectual abilities and skills are brought to the passage. This will help you to understand the Bible more fully, which in turn will give you greater benefits from your devotional reading. Bible study of this nature can be done on your own or in a small group. Many resources are available for this purpose.

'IT'S THE TRUTH – HANDLE WITH CARE!'

Paul advised Timothy to be a person who 'correctly handles the word of truth' (2 Timothy 2:15, *New International Version*). Similarly, we too must be careful to understand, interpret and use the Bible as God intended, even in our devotional reading.

God spoke to be understood. His words are now included in the Bible and were not intended to be obscure but plain to those reading them. Having understood what they are saying to us, he then expects us to respond to his initiatives and commands. Much of the Bible can be understood in a straightforward way, its meaning quite clear. But there are some passages that are not clear to us, because we are now centuries distant from the time of the original writing, and live in a quite different culture. For these cases, it is important to use the 'tools' available to help us interpret the passage correctly. These will help us to:

❋ recognise the different sorts of literature in the Bible,

* appreciate the historical background to Bible passages, and
* understand passages in their context.

When we have done this we will have gained three invaluable tools.

Different types of literature in the Bible

The Bible is really a library of books – and like most libraries contains books of differing styles of writing or 'literary forms'. Depending on the literary form, some passages require us to look beyond the literal meaning of the passage to see what it is really saying. This in no way suggests that the Bible is not inspired by God or is untrue but simply means that God speaks to us in various ways.

Six main literary forms are found in the Bible:

* *Poetry* usually expresses feelings, using symbols and figures of speech. These should not be interpreted literally. Biblical examples of poetry are found in the Psalms and the Song of Solomon.
* *Parables* are extended similes or short stories. They tend to teach a single truth or answer a single question. The details provided are often just part of the story telling, and in themselves do not have deep meaning. There are many parables in the four Gospels,

including the parable of prodigal son, the good Samaritan, the lost sheep, the sower.

❋ *Prophecy* occurs when God chooses a particular person to speak a message to his people concerning their present situation, future events or both. Old Testament examples of prophecy are found in Isaiah, Jeremiah, Hosea and Amos.

❋ *Letters* in the New Testament are written to groups of believers (like those written to the Romans, Corinthians and Galatians) and to individuals (such as the letters to Timothy and Titus). Often written in response to particular problems in a church, to get the most from them, you need to know something about the author and the reason for writing. The letters offer much challenging teaching about how to put Christianity into practice.

❋ *Historical books* of the Bible include Genesis, Joshua, Judges, 1 and 2 Kings and Ezra in the Old Testament; and the four Gospels and Acts in the New Testament. While much Old Testament history specifically describes God's dealings with the nation of Israel, there are many examples that illustrate the principles that apply to how God deals with people generally. For example, when you read about David and his relationship with Bathsheba, you see that when David sins with Bathsheba, the penalty he pays affects not only him, but brings about suffering for both his family and the nation. We can find principles that concern our relationship with God, ones especially relevant to people in leadership.

❋ *Apocalyptic writing,* vivid and poetic, forms a special category of Jewish writing. It is found in books such as Ezekiel and Daniel in the Old Testament and Revelation in the New Testament. Apocalypse means an 'unveiling' or a 'revealing'.

It is important to recognise the style of writing – and to use the rules for understanding that particular style – when thinking about the significance of particular Bible passages. An especially good resource to help you do this is *How to Read the Bible for all its Worth* by Gordon Fee and Douglas Stewart.

Understand historical background

To understand correctly the significance of many passages, you need to know some of the historical background that surrounds them. It is worth making the effort to understand the various factors (including geographical, social, religious, political and economic factors) that influence the context of the story, letter or psalm. What would it have been like for the original hearers? If we can appreciate some of that, we are in a better position to see connections between the original situations and our own experiences.

For example, before we can fully grasp the point
Jesus is making in his parable of the good Samaritan
(Luke 10:25–37), we need to appreciate the depth of
suspicion and hatred that existed between the Jews
and the Samaritans. Jews listening to Jesus would
have been astounded – indeed deeply shocked – to
hear Jesus say that the good person, or neighbour was
the Samaritan who helped the man in the ditch, rather
than the experts and guardians of God's Law who
should have been the first to demonstrate compassion.
In answering the question, 'What must I do to inherit
eternal life?' (verse 25), Jesus gave an unexpected
twist, challenging his hearers. As we attempt to put
into everyday practice the radical principle Jesus
communicated, we too will be challenged in our
discipleship. In trying to understand the depth of
feeling experienced by the original hearers when they
realised what Jesus was getting at, we begin to
appreciate fully what the principle may mean for us.

You will find helpful background information in
Bible dictionaries, commentaries and the notes found
in some Bible versions. To build up your own resource
collection, see the suggestions given in Appendix 2.

See passages in their context

Reading a short passage each day has one limitation – it

is easy to miss its wider context. To grasp the full meaning of short passages, view them within the context of surrounding verses, the whole book, and indeed the whole Bible.

To help minimise the risk of misunderstanding, follow these helpful suggestions. You may need to set aside extra time apart from your regular time with God, to implement the second and third suggestions.

SEE HOW THE PASSAGE FITS INTO THE BOOK

We have already seen that the type of literature used will provide clues to help us understand the meaning of the various passages. You also need to be aware of what precedes and follows the sentences and verses in the section you are reading as they too affect their meaning.

The most important question to keep asking as you read through the verses and paragraphs is 'what's the point of the passage?' Try to discover what the writer is saying overall and fit the section you are reading into that framework. What is the author's line of thought? Do the verses immediately preceding the section provide a clue to its meaning? Is the section laying groundwork for what follows?

To understand this well, use a version of the Bible that sets out the text in a way that shows the flow of the writer's thought, rather than one that prints each verse as a separate entity.

READ INDIVIDUAL BOOKS IN ONE SITTING

Before you start reading a book of the Bible section by section, try reading the whole book at one sitting. This will help you to fit each section into the overall plan of the book.

Most of the books in the Bible, such as the Gospels, Acts, letters in the New Testament, the narratives and shorter prophetic books in the Old Testament, are presented in a way which makes this exercise worthwhile. (It is not so useful for books like Psalms and Proverbs.)

When planning to read in this way:

❧ Set aside a block of time for uninterrupted reading. Some books will require one to two hours.

❧ Use a version of the Bible that reads easily. Paraphrases of the Bible, such as Eugene Petersen's *The Message*, are often useful for this 'overview reading'.

❧ Quickly skim through the book to acquaint yourself with its general direction. Versions with paragraph headings are helpful for this.

❧ Read the book straight through like a novel to appreciate the flow of the writing. Do not be sidetracked by details during this phase.

❧ As you read, keep in mind such questions as:

'What is the main thing the author is trying to say?'
'What are the important themes developing in the book?'
* After reading the book through, consider it as a whole.
Do any key themes apply in your situation today?
* Share your thoughts with God.

GET AN OVERVIEW OF THE WHOLE BIBLE

To get God's widest perspective try reading through the
whole Bible over a period of time. An average of three
chapters a day (and five on Sundays) will get you through
the Bible in about one year. You may prefer to read parts of
the Old Testament and New Testament alternately,
sampling the different writing styles in the Bible, rather
than reading from cover to cover. Appendix 2 suggests some
publications to guide you through the Bible in this way.

A NOTE ON UNDERSTANDING

Mark Twain is reported to have remarked, 'I'm troubled
not by the things I don't understand, but by the things I
do understand.' This idea should be applied to our
understanding of the Bible. It is not the parts of the Bible
that are difficult to understand that should bother us –
but the ones where the message is very obvious – the
parts that are easy to read and understand, but not so
easily put into practice!

Acorns & Chestnuts

EXPLORE – THE
BIBLE AND LIFE
TOGETHER

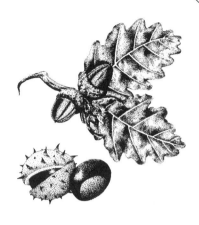

'The most important
question for me is
not, "How do I touch
people?" but, "How
do I live the word I
am speaking?" In
Jesus, no division
existed between what
he said and what he
did. Saintliness
means living
without division
between word and
action.'

HENRI NOUWEN

Having prepared to come into God's presence and after reading a section of the Bible, what can you expect to happen? If you want this time to have an impact on your life, start pondering over what you have read, then reflect upon it – in other words, explore its meaning and significance for you.

RESPOND TO THE TEXT AS A WHOLE PERSON

Reading the Bible passage and reflecting on how it relates to your life is a whole-person event.

Many of us are very good at using the analytical part of our brain – the side that enables us to use language, to understand concepts and to think logically. When we are meeting with God we certainly need to engage our minds – the minds God is renewing and transforming as part of his work in us (see 2 Corinthians 5:17, Romans 12:2) – but there is more! Jesus reminds us that the greatest commandment is to love the Lord your God 'with all your heart, soul, mind, and strength' (Mark 12:30). God wants us to love him with our *whole* being.

So, in your times with him, bring both your analytical thinking and your capacity for creativity and imagination into play through the use of symbol, metaphor, story and poem. By learning to use more of your whole-person potential when you meet with God, you are enabled to enter more fully into the riches God offers you in your daily living.

Some Christians find that *meditation* helps them achieve this. Although many people connect meditation solely with eastern religions, it is certainly not their exclusive property. Meditation that involves the whole person has its roots firmly in the biblical tradition.

What are the some of the features of the biblical view of meditation?

* Meditation is not an *emptying* of the mind, as eastern religions advocate, but a *filling*, as you dwell on God and his ways.

* Meditation is not *passive* but *active*. It involves concentrating on the passage so that you can see more clearly what God is saying to you.

* Meditation leads to *change*. As you allow God to talk to you, the Holy Spirit is enabling change to take place in your life.

* Meditation is closely related to prayer. It is *prayerful* reflection with a view to understanding and putting into practice what you learn.

God's words to Joshua help us understand meditation in this biblical sense: 'Never stop reading *The Book of the Law* he (God) gave you. Day and night you must think about what it says' (Joshua 1:8).

We may not always like the taste of food that we know is nourishing for our bodies. Similarly, we may not always like what we 'hear' when we allow God's truth to make 'its full and proper impact'. Reading a Bible passage is like taking food into our mouth, while meditation is like chewing.

Meditation

'... the activity of calling to mind, and thinking over and dwelling on, and applying to oneself, the various things that one knows about the works and way and purposes and promises of God. It is an activity of holy thought, consciously performed in the presence of God, under the eye of God, by the help of God, as a means of communion with God. Its purpose is to clear one's mental and spiritual vision of God, and let his truth make its full and proper impact on one's mind and heart...'[2]

J.I. Packer

Meditation

'... some of God's address may be sweet and we relish its refreshing savour. Some may be bitter and we will be tempted to reject it. Some may be tough to chew and we may be tempted to set it aside. Some may be like sand in our mouth and we want only to be rid of it. In meditation we begin to discover what God is saying to us at those points of our being where we are not yet what God intends us to be. This is where the bitterness, toughness, and sandiness arise. Those points are often areas of our being where we are satisfied with the status quo, comfortable in our bondage, accustomed to our brokenness. We do not want God messing around in those areas. Meditation is letting God do precisely that'![3]

M.R. Mulholland, Jr

If you will allow God to 'mess around' and change your life through the process of meditation, these guidelines on how to meditate can assist you to set this process in motion:

* ❋ Cooperate with the Holy Spirit who is at work within you.

* Use your mind.
* Allow your emotions to come into play.

Keep in step with the Holy Spirit

Whenever you come to meditate on a Bible passage, remember you are not doing all the work alone. The Holy Spirit, our foremost teacher, will enable you to grasp fully the meaning of the passage, and what it might mean for you. It is the Holy Spirit who communicates God's truth to us but that does not mean we should put our minds into 'neutral' while waiting on the Holy Spirit to illumine them! The Spirit is at work in us as we use our minds to grapple with the Bible, to understand it and relate it to our situation.

Use your mind

On page 28 three questions were identified as helpful for our reflection:

* What is the main point of the passage?
* What does the passage tell me about God?
* What might God be saying to me personally through this passage?

The first of these questions is quite straightforward. The second and third are worth describing in more detail.

What does the passage tell me about God?

Knowing people involves knowing *about* them, their characteristics and personality and how they function in different situations. So to know God, you will want to discover all you can about what he is like. When starting to explore the Bible passage, focus on God rather than yourself. Ask 'What am I discovering that is fresh or new about God that helps build up my "picture" of him?'

* Who is this God who is our creator and heavenly Father?
* Who is this Jesus who can be our Saviour and Lord?
* Who is this Holy Spirit who is Jesus' personal presence with us today?

If you are reading a passage that reveals or describes several characteristics of God, you may choose to focus on one only of these to allow adequate time to appreciate what that particular characteristic of God means for you. You can then respond in an appropriate way.

What might God be saying to me personally through this passage?

It is a life-changing experience to meet the living God, so expect him to highlight areas where you need to change or put things into practice. The following questions may assist you when seeking for possible personal messages in the passage:

* Is God *commanding* the characters in the story or the original readers to do something that I should also be doing?
* Do these same people make a *mistake* or commit a sin that I should avoid?
* Did God make a *promise* 'back then' that can still be true for me today? If so, I can respond by believing that God will continue to keep that promise in my life.
* Do any of the actions of the characters in the story, or the people discussed by the writer, provide a *good example* for me to follow?
* Does the passage yield a *principle* by which I can regulate my behaviour?

Don't expect to hear an audible voice telling you the answers to these questions. The questions are not a magical formula, but aim to help you open your mind to what God may want to teach you.

Let your emotions come into play

As you reflect on the Bible passage, take note of the emotions expressed or implied. These will contribute to your appreciation of the significance of the passage. Then try to get behind the words by asking such questions as:

* How would I *feel* if I was 'in the scene' of the passage?
* What emotions are aroused in me as I consider what God could want me to do?

Examples

❋ Consider the story of Zacchaeus (Luke 19:1-10). Imagine you are Zacchaeus. How would you feel when the crowd, knowing you well and despising you, refuses to let you see Jesus? When Jesus looks up and finds you perched in the branches of the tree overhanging the roadway? When he comes into your home?

❋ Read Matthew 6:25-34. When you read 'But more than anything else, put God's work first and do what he wants. Then the other things [like food, drink and clothing] will be yours as well' (verse 33), try to respond with your feelings, not just with your mind. Do you feel excitement? Fear? Apathy? Apprehension? Amazement?

As you begin to appreciate the range of emotions experienced by the writers or the characters in a passage, you will be more likely to see the fuller significance of the situation for you today. When you understand a passage *and* its emotional impact upon you, you begin to be 'on target' to allow God to work out his plans *for* you and *with* you.

Acknowledge your feelings as you read, accept them as part of you, and share them with God. They are a stepping stone to your next step of obedience – and to developing a closer relationship with your loving God.

NOTE: To help you use more of your creative potential in your times with God, Chapter 8 has a variety of methods that you could use to allow him to communicate to you as a total person.

CONNECTING THE BIBLE TO EVERYDAY LIFE

During the time we spend meditating on the various Bible passages, we not only get to know God better but discover the significance of God's word for our lives. So look for things *which arise from the passage* that are *specific, realistic* and *relevant* to you, then ask God to show you how you can put into practice your discoveries.

Is the connection specific?

Look out for something specific that you can do, rather than for something vague and general. Does your attitude to someone or something need to change? For example, you might ask for grace to be patient and self-controlled when dealing with a particular difficult person, instead of asking for all the 'fruit of the Spirit' (Galatians 5:22-23, *GNB*) to be developed in your life today. Or, you could ask for inner peace in the morning when you are trying frantically to get your family off to school and yourself to work on time.

Is the connection realistic?

Be alert for something you could achieve with God's help. If reading from Acts for example, the verse '...you will tell everyone about me...' (Acts 1:8) might catch your attention. You might be tempted to pray in a vague way for opportunities to witness to people but a more realistic prayer would be to ask for an opportunity to talk about God with one or two people at work this week.

Is the connection relevant?

Does the passage bring to mind something that seems relevant to your life and current situation? Remember that God has put you in a particular place and wants you to be obedient where you are, not where you're not! Being relevant means looking for things that you can do as an individual without being *individualistic* (= self-centred rather than being in relationship with others) and personal but not *privatised* (= when your Christian faith is a private concern which fails to relate to the life of wider society).

Does the connection arise from the passage?

If a thought arises from outside the passage you are meditating upon which seems to require action, how do you check whether it is consistent with the intent of the passage? To ensure that your proposed action is in line with what God would want you to do, check it against these questions:

* Is there a clear link between the content of the passage and what you think you should do?

* Is your proposed action in line with the central thrust of the passage?

* Even though it arises from the passage, is your proposed action consistent with the wider teaching of the Bible?

* Do the big themes of the Bible and issues in society around you (see 'Appreciate the full scope of the Bible' on page 77) raise concerns in you about how you are applying the Bible to your life? Test this out by asking if this will affect your attitude and action towards, for example, the poor, exploited, suffering or powerless.

'I am no believer in getting guidance from opening the Bible at random and suddenly spotting a guidance verse, but there are rare and very special occasions when a verse of Scripture, occurring in the regular course of one's reading, suddenly fits like a key to a lock. Of far greater importance is an understanding of the broad principles of scriptural teaching. But when that is not neglected, and when there has been a background of regular and faithful prayer, the occasional gem occurring at the right time and the right place, cannot be denied its relevance, its confirmation and its comfort.'[4]

John Laird

GET INCREASED MILEAGE FROM YOUR BIBLICAL REFLECTION

The following additional ideas will help you get more out of your time of thinking and reflecting on a passage. They will assist you to understand the passage better, and prepare you for making the 'jump' from the Bible to your life today.

Recognise your 'filters'

Whenever you read the Bible, you bring to it a whole package of ideas originating from your personal and social background. These colour your understanding of what is written and may cause you to filter the words you read, maybe missing much of what they are really saying. There are three common 'filters': cultural, doctrinal, and personal.

Cultural filter

There is most likely an immense cultural gap between your social environment and that of the Middle Eastern cultures in which the Bible originated. There certainly is for me, with my middle class, European, New Zealand upbringing. Members of the biblical cultures would consider me, for example, to be very affluent and would struggle to understand what they perceive to be my excessive 'individualism'. They would be surprised at how I define 'my family', and the lifestyle of my wife and teenage sons. They would be amazed at the technology that I take for granted in many areas of my life.

My values and attitudes and much of my behaviour are deeply ingrained because I am part of my particular culture, and I'm often unaware of how they influence me. This 'cultural filter' affects my interpretation of the Bible in significant ways. The books of the Bible were written into specific cultural and social environments that were quite different from mine. When I appreciate this fact, the message of the Bible may become more dynamic. Here are two striking examples of the difference:

* *The relationship between the people of Israel and God.* To understand this we need to be aware that their worship of God (theology) was no mere 'spiritual' matter. It was closely related to both their community (social) life and their stewardship of the land God that provided for them (economic aspect). These three areas were intimately interrelated for Israelites of Old Testament times but we usually see them as separate entities. Hence, we may fail to see that God intends our worship to affect such things as our work and use of money, our sexuality and our involvement with our community. Appreciating this difference between the Israelite and our own cultures helps open the door for a better understanding of much of the teaching of the Old Testament.

* *The impact of Jesus' accepting attitude towards women in the Palestine of his day.* Jesus' attitude to women was extremely confronting as the prevailing cultural attitude usually relegated women to the status of 'second class citizen'. Social changes in the industrialised world in the last hundred years or so

mean we take for granted the right of women to own property, earn a living, gain an education, etc. None of these things were the norm in New Testament times. It is little wonder that when Jesus spoke to the Samaritan woman at the well (John 4:5-42) and Mary sat at Jesus' feet to learn from him (Luke 10:38-42), that his disciples and others saw these encounters as radical acts.

Doctrinal filter

Local church fellowships tend to emphasise certain aspects of the Bible message. Each will have a distinctive understanding of the Bible's teaching such as following a particular tradition on baptism, the involvement of Christians in 'the world' or the work of the Holy Spirit. When we come to the Bible, we may seek to reinforce those views in every passage we read, unaware we are doing this. We need to be open to what God's Holy Spirit wants to teach us. At times we may have to give up views, dearly held, on matters where we believed we had the authoritative position. (Always carefully check your discoveries with others, to confirm that you are learning accurately!)

Personal filter

When meeting with God you bring along your own hopes, power or lack of power, fears and expectations of what you want from this relationship. These will influence what you see in Bible passages. For example, if you are in need of clear direction – for your career, marriage, lifestyle, etc. – you may bring your desire for this to your times with God, seeing 'guidance' in Bible passages, even if this is not actually present in the passage.

Your 'in-built' cultural, doctrinal and personal filters mean that you need to proceed with some care in making a jump from the pages of the Bible to your situation today. Recognise that the filters exist, even if you cannot easily identify them. Humility before God is essential – realise that your mind has limitations, and thank God that he can help you in your understanding.

Appreciate the full scope of the Bible

Too often Christians fail to allow the message of the Bible to speak for itself. Be aware of the *full* scope of the Bible's themes and principles. Allow your thinking and response to God to be s-t-r-e-t-c-h-e-d, rather than trying to squeeze God into the limited framework you have, resulting from your incomplete knowledge of him.

The Bible *does* address itself to questions of personal lifestyle and holiness, but it also addresses issues and concerns larger than you and your personal world.

Coping with daily living (like temptation, fear, bad habits, relationship difficulties) is easier for Christians when they see their lives in the broad perspective of God's character and work. Read Colossians 1:15-20 to appreciate the scope of God's creation, and his plan, through Jesus Christ, to bring the whole universe back to himself – 'everything in heaven and on earth, everything seen and unseen, including all forces and powers, and all rulers and authorities' (verse 16).

So come to recognise the big themes of the Bible: sin, conflict (people against God, people against nature, people against other people, people against themselves), death and reconciliation. Notice how often the Bible addresses the 'big issues' of human existence – economics, poverty, injustice, oppression, war – and highlights God's people (the church) as his agents for change! Keep this wide vision in mind. It will help you grasp the breadth of what God might be saying to you in any Bible passage you explore.

God speaks to groups, as well as individuals

When you ask, 'What is God saying to me through this passage?' be aware that much of the Bible was written not to individuals, but to groups of believers. A passage may be addressing you as a member of a group of Christians such as your local church or Christian fellowship and not as an individual.

For example, Paul wrote most of his letters to particular churches: 'to all God's people who belong to Christ Jesus at Philippi' (Philippians 1:1); 'to God's people who live in Colossae' (Colossians 1:2). So where he writes 'you', he is generally addressing Christians *as a group* rather than as a collection of individuals. This casts interesting light on some of the commands that Christians often apply to themselves as individuals. For example, the armour of God (Ephesians 6:13-18) is something for Christians to put on *together* to make sure they are well-equipped for the spiritual battle they are involved in *as a community of God's people* seeking to accomplish the mission to which God has called them.

Passages like this may provide challenges for individuals, but their full meaning goes beyond the individual application. So be open to allowing God to highlight an area for change or action that you need to work on with the members of the Christian groups of which you are part.

6

Pohutakawa

RESPOND
TO GOD

'Prayer requires
utmost attention on
our part. Attention
to God is meditation
on his ways and
observation of his
workings, and as we
learn more of his
works and ways, we
frame our lives
accordingly.'

C A R R O L L   S I N C O X

E xploring the Bible is an important part of meeting with God. It may be thought provoking and enjoyable, but unless we allow our lives to be affected by it, it will have limited value. Reflection must always be followed by response and so our worship of the three-in-one God (Father, Son and Holy Spirit) must find its completion in changed lives.

God delights in our praises as we rejoice in who he is and what he has done. However, he only accepts them as we continue to demonstrate through our actions, attitudes, relationships and priorities that we are giving him glory and honour every day. Some of the strongest words of the Old Testament are those spoken by God through his prophets to people whose worship failed to reflect their daily living. Note the words of Isaiah, 'I am disgusted with... I cannot stand your... festivals...'; Amos, 'I hate your religious festivals... I will not accept your offerings... Stop your noisy songs...'; Micah 'What he [the Lord] requires of us is this: to do what is just, to show constant love, and to live in humble fellowship with our God.' (Isaiah 1:10-17; Amos 5:21-24; Micah 6:6-8, *GNB*)

Paul the Apostle pointed out to early Christians that right living is worship:

> Dear friends, God is good. So I beg you to offer your
> bodies to him as a living sacrifice, pure and pleasing.
> That's the most sensible way to serve God (Romans 12:1).

Two important aspects for Christians seeking to respond to God, *prayer* and *steps of practical action,* are really two sides of the same coin. Here we discuss them separately.

RESPOND TO GOD – IN PRAYER
What is prayer?

What pictures and ideas come to mind as you think about prayer?

* A small child at bedtime praying 'God bless Mummy, God bless Daddy and I hope it's sunny tomorrow, so I can play outside. Amen.'
* A devout churchgoer kneeling at a pew reading a prayer from a book.
* A young man trapped in a car accident pleading, 'God, if you get me out of here alive, I'll do anything you want me to do!'
* A preacher firing up his congregation with words like, 'the more you pray in faith, the more God will give you. Health? Wealth? Name it – and claim it!'

'Prayer' can mean many things and you will be able to add to these examples from your own experience. Prayer is something we do when we talk to God but it is often a one-way conversation – we pour out our hearts to God, telling him everything, sometimes presenting him with a 'shopping list' of all the things we want him to do for us.

But what of prayer as life-creating and life-changing as described by Richard Foster?

To pray is to change. Prayer is the central avenue God uses to transform us. If we are unwilling to change we will abandon prayer as a noticeable characteristic of our lives.[5]

Does this sound different from the ideas you have of prayer? In this kind of prayer, Christians come with an open heart, willing the Holy Spirit to challenge them where change is needed, and open to hearing God's message to them. When we pray in this way we are 'listening' to God as well as talking to him. As we allow room for God's Holy Spirit to communicate with us in this way, prayer takes on a transforming role to change us and deepen our relationship with him.

True prayer is simply spending time with God, getting to know him more and more, to appreciate him and his perspective for our lives. A Christian saint, Teresa of Avila, wrote many centuries ago that 'Prayer is nothing else than being on terms of friendship with God'. In this sense, prayer is:

* An expression of *faith*. We are saying to God, 'I trust you with my life. I want to understand more of your view of things'.

* An expression of *love*. We are saying to God, 'It's because you love me that I am able to love you, and submit myself to learn of your will for me. What do you want me to do?'

* An act of *discipleship*. We are saying to God, 'Just as Jesus initiated the reign of your kingdom in our world, so I want to be part of that and see your will done.'

As we express our faith, love and willingness to serve in this way, we receive a gift from God – he graciously chooses to release his power to us. God delights in the growing sense of community that springs up between him and his people. Prayer enables us to become co-partners with the Lord of creation in the work of his kingdom. It is much more than a one-way conversation!

Prayer

Archbishop Temple is reported as saying, in effect, 'When people stop praying, coincidences stop.' In my experience, the words can also be reversed: 'When people keep on praying, "coincidences" become significant'.[6]

John Laird

Develop your ability to pray

We often feel inadequate when it comes to prayer because it seems such a mysterious activity!

The best way to learn to pray is by starting to pray!

There is no better place to start than to study Jesus' model prayer. His disciples must have felt just like us because they asked him to teach them how to pray. In his response (Matthew 6:5-15) Jesus included the words we know as the 'Lord's Prayer'.

This, then, is how you should pray:

> *'Our Father in heaven:*
> *May your holy name be honoured;*
> *may your Kingdom come;*
> *may your will be done on earth as it is in heaven.*
> *Give us today the food we need.*
> *Forgive us the wrongs we have done,*
> *as we forgive the wrongs that others have done to us.*
> *Do not bring us to hard testing,*
> > *but keep us safe from the Evil One.*

(Matthew 6:9-13, GNB)

The teaching of Jesus highlights key components to build into *our* praying.

❧ *Right attitudes* play the essential part in prayer (Matthew 6:5-8) and the words we use must reflect those attitudes. We must first recognise *who God is* – 'our Father in heaven'. As we spend time acknowledging him and his presence, this will lead naturally into praise.

We need to examine whether we are *sincere.* When not seeking something solely for ourselves but seeking time to give God his rightful place in our lives, we will find that prayer gradually becomes active. This will occur when we submit to the holy one, allowing him to fulfil his purposes through us.

* By following Jesus' pattern we soon realise that prayer is as much *listening to God* as talking to him. For example, when we pray 'may your will be done...', we should pause and ask how this might be so – 'how might I be involved in doing God's will today?' This sort of reflection becomes a natural part of prayer as we take Jesus' advice to his disciples seriously.

* *Invite God to provide for our physical needs* ('our daily bread') *and our spiritual needs* ('forgive us the wrongs we have done') to demonstrate his grace to us. Acknowledge the spiritual realities of our world ('keep us safe from the Evil One'). Recognise in humility that God is the ultimate provider of all things.

Frameworks for prayer

The 'Lord's Prayer' is a helpful structure for learning the discipline of prayer. As well, the following prayer frameworks provide useful guidelines for ways to spend time talking and listening to God.

ACTS

Adoration – praise God for who he is and what he has done.

Confession – admit your sin and failure and ask God for his forgiveness.

Thanksgiving – say 'thanks, God' for what he is doing in your life and in the lives of others.

Supplication – pray for others and their needs, as well as your own.

Five 'A's

Approach – prepare to meet God, and be still in his presence.

Acknowledge who God is, recognising his character and qualities.

Appreciate – thank God for the ways in which he demonstrates his goodness.

Admit – confess your failures to God.

Ask – make your requests known to God for yourself and others.

Praying for others

Praying for other people – often called 'intercession' or 'intercessory prayer' – is an important part of our response to God. It does *not* mean that we tell God how to deal with other people, assuming we know their needs. Rather, it means sharing concerns consciously with God,

secure in the certainty that he is in control of
everything. Intercession then is a way of inviting God
to intervene in the lives of the people we name.

How do pray for other people? Here are some
stimulating ideas to put into practice in your regular
special time with God and others you can use during
your daily activities:

* When you feel God prompting you strongly to pray
  for particular people, pause and talk to him about
  them. Ask, 'Lord, what can I pray for them?' If you
  have no clear sense of what to pray about, say
  something like, 'God, I don't know why these
  people have come to mind, but wherever they are,
  please assure them of your presence at this time.'
  But do not base your prayer for others *solely* on
  'God's prompting', for that is neither responsible
  nor satisfying.

* Request newsletters from Christian individuals,
  organisations and mission societies; and/or check
  out their internet websites. These provide up-to-
  date information for informed prayer. Develop a
  photo prayer-file in conjunction with this.

* Internet websites provide a wide range of regular
  summaries of what God is doing in different areas
  of the world and the church. This technology can
  be used effectively to pray for others in an informed

way. However, don't be tempted to equate time spent
'surfing the net' with quality prayer!

❊ Use the various prayers found throughout the Bible as
your basis for prayer. Relate their insights to those for
whom you are praying. For example:

> Psalms 13, 16, 46, 118 (see also 'Praying the
> Psalms' on page 149)
> Paul's prayers in Philippians 1:3-11 and Colossians
> 1:3-14.

The prayer Jesus prayed in John 17.

❊ When praying for particular people, use items you
associate with them to 'trigger' your prayers, such as a
photo of relatives or friends, a child's toy, your church
newsletter or a view across your city. Use daily
mundane tasks, like hanging out washing or ironing, as
a catalyst for prayer, praying for the person belonging
to the item of clothing. When reading your mail, pray
for the person who has written to you. Pray about news
items when reading the newspapers or watching news
reports on TV. Or, when drinking from your favourite
coffee mug, pray for the person who gave it to you.
Don't just rely on visual triggers. Use sounds such as
music playing, a child crying, a siren blaring, or smells
and tastes as a stimulus for your prayers. While
walking, use the places you pass as a cue for your
prayers. Remember too that unattractive things can

just as easily spur you to prayer, as can more
pleasant images. They remind us of the presence of
pain, evil and sin.

These fleeting reminders of particular people during
the day may result in brief sentence prayers – but
they effectively bring these people and concerns
into the creative circle of the power of God's love.

A prayer language – a valuable gift

Sometimes, God gives particular people the gift of a
special 'prayer language' through his Holy Spirit. This
language of the spirit, rather than the mind, is not
learned. If used in a public church meeting, expect
God to give another the ability to interpret the
message given so that everyone can benefit from it.
But in private, the gift of 'tongues' does not need an
interpreter. If you have been given this gift, it may give
you a greater freedom of spirit than what you have
known previously, enabling you to praise God from
the depths of your being. Or when you do not know
how to pray for a particular person, it may help you to
pray on their behalf.

As with other gifts from God, this gift does not
appear to be for everyone. Those who receive it are no
more spiritual than those without it, but if God has
graciously given you this gift, it is important to

exercise it. However, keep in mind that the most important thing is to be obedient to God in everyday life, to the Giver rather than the gift.

Resources for prayer

We think of prayer as talking to or with God in an unstructured two-way conversation. Here are some other ways to enhance your experience of prayer:

Written prayers: Reflect on your discoveries about God and how you can respond. You may like to write down your thoughts in the traditional form of a prayer, a letter or even an e-mail to God.

Using prepared prayers: Many prepared prayers are available. Draw on them. These often help with things that are difficult to express, expanding your vision of what you can pray about, making your prayer time more meaningful.

Books containing collections of prayers range from very old prayers to contemporary styles of expression. Some churches have official service books that contain a range of prayers for many occasions (such as the Anglican *Book of Common Prayer* or its modern counterpart, *A Prayer Book for Australia*). Check out the prayer resources available in various Christian bookshops.

Prayer and music: God's gift of music can be used

effectively for prayer and many songs and hymns are in the form of prayers. The Bible has numerous examples where people express themselves through songs and music. In several of the Psalms (the prayer and hymnbook of the nation of Israel), the writers encouraged the Israelites to 'sing a new song to the Lord' (Psalm 33:3, 96:1, 98:1, 149:1). They knew that music greatly helps people to express their responses to God both emotionally and with their minds.

So use music and song as aids for expressing yourself in prayer. Experiment with the following suggestions:

* Sing a song or hymn which says what you want to say to God – whether boisterous praise or subdued confession, expressions of quiet confidence or a questioning mood.
* Silently meditate on the words of a song as you listen, making its words and ideas your own.
* Rewrite the words of a hymn to fit your situation – or create a new verse for an existing song.
* Write your own song of response to God.
* Use the Psalms to express yourself (see 'Praying the Psalms', p. 149).

Both song and music are a God-given resource. Use your God-given creativity to make them a significant part of your prayer-expression!

RESPOND TO GOD – IN PRACTICAL ACTION

When you ask the question, 'What is God saying to me personally?' you are really asking, 'What does God want to do in my life and through me, that will have some effect in the lives of people around me?'

If something fruitful is to result from your time with God, it will need to be expressed in practical ways. Chapter 5 gave an outline of questions we should ask when we are looking for direction for living God's way. You may wish to review this checklist before you read this next section to make sure that what you think the Bible passages are saying to you is 'on target'.

How does the Bible help us change?

There is no magical way to ensure that the more you read the Bible and pray, the more you will grow in your relationship with God.

We all know the power of words. Remember the childhood chant, 'sticks and stones may break my bones but words will never hurt me' – we soon learned that words *can* hurt us deeply. Affirming words encourage us, thoughtless words annoy us, angry words make us defensive, comforting words support us. It is not the word itself that produces a response in us; the word is merely a tool for communicating meaning. But words are powerful

– they reveal the mind of the writer or speaker and draw out thoughts and emotions in the reader or hearer.

So too with the words in the Bible – the words found there help us more than any others to become like Jesus Christ. As you read them, you open yourself to the dynamic power of God's Holy Spirit, who takes those words and uses them to challenge, rebuild, and mould your life. And while you are examining the words of a Bible passage, you often discover *the passage* is examining *you*! The writer of the New Testament letter to the Hebrews put this vividly:

> *What God has said isn't only alive and active! It is sharper than any double-edged sword. His word can cut through our spirits and souls and through our joints and marrow until it discovers the desires and thoughts of our hearts (Hebrews 4:12)*

The words of the Bible become God's word to us as we see God revealing himself and his purposes for his creation through them. They help us understand why Jesus is called by the special name, 'the Word of God': Jesus shows us God's very nature (John 1:1-18), communicating God's personality and purposes to people.

God's words in the Bible – and supremely, Jesus his living Word – actively bring about transformation in our lives as we allow them to talk to us in our various circumstances. When we desire to read and understand the Bible, we become open to putting what we read into practice in our lives. This is our springboard to growing in faith, knowledge and the love of God, his Son Jesus, and his Holy Spirit. The way we express this is through our obedience to God as he calls us to do particular things for him in his world.

Walking by Faith

When seeking to walk by faith there are "undercurrents of deep perplexity and uncertainty as to guidance for the future... It is often out of such experiences that the best guidance comes, but one must patiently await God's time, for guidance is part of the trend of life and is not merely the emotion of the moment. That which is to be born must come to maturity and not be enforced prematurely. 'If it seem slow wait for it; it will surely come, it will not delay'   (Habakkuk 2:3)."[7]

John Laird

Areas in which God helps us to change

As we develop a close relationship with God, we allow him to work at a process of re-forming us. This is often called 'spiritual formation', but it actually brings change to all aspects of our lives. 'Spiritual growth' is not merely an increase in our knowledge of God, or how much time we give to 'spiritual activities'. It is expected that over time we will see growth in every part of our life, and as a lifetime activity!

One writer has put it this way:

> *'Spiritual growth ... is a process of becoming more integrated, more whole. It is a process of bringing into harmony with one another my mind (intellectual belief), my heart (emotions), my will (choices), and my actions (expressed through my physical body) ... if the goals of such integration of mind, emotions, will and action is a greater freedom to love and serve God in his world and in others, then we are indeed talking about healthy Christian spirituality.*[8]

What are some of the specific areas in which you can expect to see changes and growth?

Thinking Understanding our faith as Christians, and how this affects every aspect of our life.

Feelings The range and quality of the feelings (emotions) we have towards God, ourselves, others and God's creation.

Tendencies Practical demonstrations of the fruit of the Holy Spirit (Galatians 5:22-23) should be able to be seen more and more consistently in our everyday lives.

Self-esteem When we know we are accepted by God we are free to accept ourselves fully.

Relationships Both our desire and ability to enter into caring relationships will reflect the example of Jesus, enabling us to love our neighbours as we love our [God-accepted] selves (Luke 10:27).

Development of special gifts Learn to appreciate and use the special spiritual gift(s) which God has given you and other individuals to enable the Church to fulfil its mission.

Responsibility Accept the responsibilities of membership of God's 'kingdom-community' – by becoming involved in service (ministry) both within the Church and in wider society.[9]

Now think about which of these seven areas in your life need change and growth? Talk this over with God – and be open to the insights he gives! Keep these especially in mind as you meet regularly with him in the coming weeks.

Take heart!

As you try to show your love for God in obedient action, remember that you can trust him to make himself clear to you. Keep praying! Ask God to enable you to persevere and to take away any desire to act in ways that are unpleasing to him so that gradually you become changed into the likeness of his son, Jesus Christ.

Growing into Christian maturity – that is becoming more like Jesus Christ – is a life-long journey. Being open to God's direction requires small steps of obedience and occasionally, more 'dramatic' ones. God will not expect more from you than what he knows you can give. Other Christians can provide you with help and encouragement in this area (see Chapter 7 for suggestions).

Guidance

Wise decisions are a compound of experience, courage, intuitiveness, imagination, knowledge of the facts, willingness to take risks and awareness of the possibility of failure. Sometimes our decisions will be mistaken and wrong. What should we do then? The important thing is to be sufficiently honest to admit frankly that a mistake has been made and not to bluff it out and go ahead in pride, but to be willing to go back and start again, even if it involves some embarrassment. The man who never made a mistake never made anything, and there are times when we have to take the plunge in faith and hope, and strike out for the other side of the river.

When the prayer life is active and steadfastly maintained day by day and over the years, there is a great safeguard against foolish and ill-judged decisions. With growth and spiritual maturity, a healthy instinct can be developed, intuitively warning of danger or prompting to go ahead. Similarly, a constant, systematic and well-balanced daily reading of Scripture and meditation helps to shape modes of thought and implants certain broad principles of right and wrong. Scripture is largely biographical and the constant study of the triumphs and disasters of the men and women represented is immensely instructive.[10]   *John Laird*

Recognise God's voice

While it might be your wish that God speak directly to you about decisions, this is rarely the way he chooses to communicate. So how can you be sure that when you seek direction for your life, it is God who is speaking to you?

❋ Most of what God requires of you – in your character and actions – is set out clearly in the Bible, either in detail or in principle. So for much of the time, you will recognise God's voice through your thoughtful reading of the Scriptures. For example, when you find aspects of positive character development highlighted in a passage of the Bible, you should not need a special voice from heaven to tell you that it is God who is instructing you.

❋ Where the Bible does not deal directly with an issue, God wants you to use your mind and will to decide what to think or how to act, using his values and principles as the basis for your decision. Both your mind and will should be open to the teaching of the Holy Spirit, but use the following questions to check your sense of direction from God in such cases:

  • Is it in harmony with the teaching and principles of the Bible as it 'teaches the truth, corrects error, re-sets the direction of our lives and trains us in good living' (2 Timothy 3:16, J.B. Phillips' translation)? Or, does it conflict in some way?

- Do you have inner peace about the rightness of the decision? Does it 'feel right' – or do you feel uneasy about it? But beware – sometimes feeling uneasy is simply fear of the unknown or a lack of readiness for change.
- Do other people agree with its rightness? Check it out with several mature Christians whose views you respect.

Positive answers to all three of these questions are more likely to indicate God's direction than an affirmative answer to just one of them.

Get your feelings into perspective

God has never promised to lead us by our inner feelings. Instead, his Holy Spirit gives us the wisdom to understand and obey God's purposes (see, for example, John's Gospel 14:15-27; 16:12-15). But we have been given a mind and emotions and we need to use *both* fully.

Problems arise when we choose to be guided by only one of these. Balance is needed. Some Christians make decisions because they *feel* right, failing to check them against more objective criteria, like checking out what the Bible may say or discussing the matter with others. They then wonder why things do not work out well. Others choose a course of action because it seems the logical and right way to go, but their emotions do not endorse the decision. They may also end up wondering why the outcome is less than satisfactory.

* Sometimes, although you know God is speaking to you about an issue, you feel uncomfortable about it, especially if it is an emotionally sensitive area for you (for example, choice of marriage partner, the use of your possessions, your attitude towards a certain person). Then it is important to respond with your mind and not allow your feelings to dominate. God will confirm in various ways whether your mind has directed you correctly. This will make you more confident about obeying him in future – you will realise that in his longing for you to become more like Jesus, God wants the very best for you.

* On the other hand, when strong feelings prompt you to do something, first check them by the more objective standards mentioned above, before proceeding on a course of action.

Many Christians struggle to gain a balanced perspective on 'guidance'. If you need more help in understanding how God guides, read one of the books suggested in Appendix 3.

Learn to recognise God's presence in your daily living

Details of your everyday life are important to God and you will find the impact of your special time with him flows out into your daily activity. There's an art to 'remaining in the presence of God daily' – and Brother Lawrence, a 17th century monk, provides us with insights into developing this 'art'.

Brother Lawrence was a simple man who made marked progress in his spiritual life after his conversion to Christ. A key factor was his attitude – he did everything in the presence of God. He saw little division between his work in the noise and clutter of the monastery kitchen and the daily times especially set aside for worship and prayer. One of his colleagues wrote:

> *He [Brother Lawrence] told me ... that we might accustom ourselves to a continual conversation with Him [God] with freedom and simplicity. That we need only to recognise God intimately present with us to address ourselves to Him every moment...* [11]

As we make a conscious effort to use our daily routines to develop fellowship with God – walking, driving or riding to work; having a bath; performing daily chores, we, like Brother Lawrence, will make progress in our Christian lives and relationships. These prayer times will become more like a conversation of friend with friend – and you can tell God about the happenings of your day or ask for his help in a specific situation. These may be brief expressions of thankfulness springing from a grateful heart or confessions of failure when you realise you have displeased God and need to start afresh. When people come to mind, pray for them. Gradually you will discover the ways that best suit you.

At first there will be long periods where you do not consciously include God in your activities. These intervals will grow shorter as you work at recognising his presence with you. When you develop this art you will find, as did Brother Lawrence, that you are growing closer to God. Your special time with God, where you read the Bible and pray, will become increasingly integrated into all of your life.

KEEP TRACK OF YOUR JOURNEY WITH GOD

In what ways are you making progress as a Christian? How have you grown in your relationship with God over the past week, or month, or year? Review your Christian growth regularly to see what God has communicated to you, and how you have responded. Your reviews will be more effective if you write things down in a folder or notebook as they happen.

Expressing yourself in writing often will clarify what

you are praying for or what specific action you should take.

These three suggestions may help you to maintain a record of your growth:

Set goals for action

Set yourself goals for change and action, noting them down, and evaluating them regularly. When you achieve targets, this will lead to thanksgiving. And if not, you may need to modify them or confess your failure, asking for God's help in meeting them.

Keep a prayer diary

Use a notebook (perhaps divided into seven sections for the days of the week) to record the names of people, organisations, or situations you wish to pray for. Note down specific requests and items – and God's answers! You will be encouraged and excited to see how God has been working.

Write a journal

Many people find that keeping a *journal* helps them in their spiritual growth. A journal is simply a notebook where you record your thoughts and feelings as you proceed in the Christian life. The act of writing may help you to 'get in touch' with things that are deep within you, to tune into what is going on between God and yourself. As you jot down your thoughts and feelings, your thinking will become clearer, and your journal entries will encourage accurate recall later on.

❋ Regular journal writing can be a beneficial discipline. 'Journalling' is a learning process, so experiment with what works best for you, with your own personality and preferences. It is not essential to write every day and a few lines at a time will be sufficient.

❋ Your journal is a personal record of discoveries about yourself in relation to God and his world and can include any number of aspects:

- a response to a Bible passage
- a description of a personal event
- your reaction to a situation
- insights into a person's behaviour
- encouragement received
- a personal 'stock-taking'
- impressions after meeting someone
- recording a dream
- a prayer you have discovered or a song you have composed
- a failure recognised
- clarifying a confusion
- forming a question you need answered
- a dialogue with God or part of yourself etc.

❋ A journal is a little different to diaries; diaries tend to be records of events, while journals are more often a reflection on the meaning of those events. In your journal writing, try to move from the description of events to a reflection on its meaning for you, its impact on you as a whole person. In other words, use both sides of your brain! (see page 62)

❋ Your journal is a private record – between God and you (so try to keep it away from prying eyes!). Because there is no need to impress anyone, try to be honest with yourself in your writing. However, there may be times when you and others could benefit from sharing your discoveries with each another (see Chapter 7 – 'Share your discoveries').

❋ What you write may not seem important at the time, but may prove valuable as you look back over the development of your relationship with God. Regularly review your journal and use these times as opportunities for further reflection – and ongoing writing!

❋ Many journal-writers use a bound exercise book (A5 size is good). Or, you may wish to experiment with writing directly onto your computer, unless this inhibits your creativity and reflection.

❋ The most famous example of a journal is the book of Psalms in the Bible. In the Psalms, we see some of God's people in Israel expressing themselves to God as they experience the whole range of emotions and

circumstances. You will find helpful ideas for the
development of your journal there (see p. 149)
Appendix 3 suggests books to help you further your
journal writing.

RESPOND TO GOD – WITHOUT FIGHTING YOUR PERSONALITY!

There is no one prescribed method of spiritual
development. Each of us is different in our preferred
ways of approaching God, communicating with him,
expressing our worship, and experiencing his presence
and guidance.

Our personalities influence very much the ways we
feel comfortable in expressing our Christian faith.
Becoming aware of your personality will help you
discover the most helpful means of spiritual expression
for you. There are a number of personality and
temperament tests available to help you indicate your
'type' (the Myers-Briggs Type Indicator (MBTI) is
perhaps the best known) and so understand yourself
better. For example,

❋ people whose temperament is more inward looking,
and who enjoy time to themselves, find it easier to
have extended times of solitude with God than
those who 'recharge their batteries' by being with
others.

111

* those who 'naturally' like to have things settled and orderly are more comfortable with a structured way of expressing their friendship with God – a daily routine is not difficult for them! Those who like to live more spontaneously, however, want flexibility and variety in the way they express their commitment.

* some feel more comfortable when their relationship with God is clearly seen to be relevant to the 'here and now'. They want to discover practical insights that are immediately applicable. In contrast, others are happier seeing the bigger, longer-term picture of God's reign over creation, like his justice and peace.

* some people ('thinkers') tend to be analytical and logical, and find Bible study attractive. Others ('feelers') find the Bible takes on a new focus for them as it helps them develop a deeper intimacy with God.

Do not fight who you are! If you try to model yourself on one pattern, you may be unnaturally squeezed into a shape that inhibits you, rather than freeing you to be more truly yourself with God. This is one of the reasons that this handbook has attempted to present a variety of ways of approaching our times with God, and of responding to him.

However, we also need to find the balance that comes when we consciously develop our weaker areas. If we prefer solitude (being alone in God's presence), we may need to work on responding to God by taking appropriate practical forms of service. Or, if we are a more 'activist' sort of Christian, we will benefit from discovering the spiritual strength drawn from taking 'time out' from doing things for God.

One model for this balance comes from Jesus Christ himself. If you read the Gospels carefully, you will note a certain rhythm to his life. Times of busyness are followed by times for reflection and prayer which energise him for the next period of busy service. That rhythm is well worth copying, though each of us will respond to God through reflection, prayer and practical action in different ways.

Appendix 3 provides suggestions for finding resources to help you appreciate the place personality plays in your response to God.

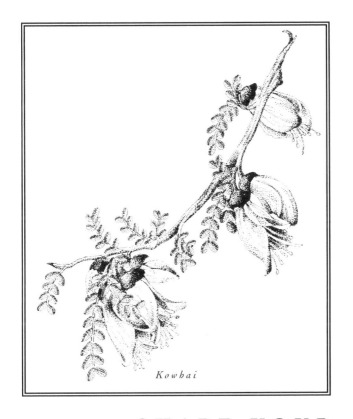

Kowhai

SHARE YOUR
DISCOVERIES

'The gospel is not a
purely personal
matter. It has a
social dimension. It
is a communal
affair.'

ROBERT BANKS

So far, this handbook has concentrated on helping you develop a personal regular encounter with God. This is important, because salvation in Jesus Christ is personal and discipleship must be pursued individually.

But equally, none of us lives in isolation from others – we are all members of families, towns, nations, even the international community. God calls us to witness to our relationship with him to the people in these communities, through our words, attitudes and actions.

The Bible also stresses that the Church – God's special community of believers – is vital to this. We have a special link with other Christians because we are all members of the same family of God. Hence we find metaphors of God's people in the Bible such as, 'the body of Christ', 'the family of God', 'a holy nation', and 'the chosen race'. The New Testament demonstrates that lone Christians are the exception rather than the rule!

Whether or not you like your fellow Christians, you belong to each other. You need them in order to grow – and they need you! *Accountability* to others for your spiritual growth, and *responsibility* for the growth of other Christians, are core values for life in God's new community. If you need convincing about whether or not this accountability and responsibility applies to you, collect all the 'one another' statements you can find in the

New Testament and compare them. Start with 'love one another' (1 John 3:11), 'pray for one another' (James 5:16), 'care for one another' (1 Corinthians 12:25-26), 'show hospitality to one another' (1 Peter 4:9), but there are many more!

This mutual dependence (or 'interdependence') can be expressed in a variety of ways. Here are some to help you as you start to grow in your relationship with God:

SHARE WITH A FRIEND

Share your special time with God with a friend (or two). If possible, make this a regular event – meet whenever you have some spare time – before work, once a week, during a mealtime.

* Use the four-step method (Chapter 2) or experiment with other methods (Chapter 8). Share the insights God gives to each of you. To put several minds together is more productive and enriching than one.

* Share your concerns and the ways you put what you are learning into practice. Encourage your friend(s) to check on your progress.

* Pray together, and for each other.

* Contract to pray for each other regularly between meeting times.

HELP OTHERS DEVELOP THEIR DEVOTIONAL TIMES

Whether you have just started your Christian journey or been on it for some time, you too can help and encourage others. Pray for – and took out for – opportunities to share your discoveries. Two possibilities come immediately to mind:

Fellow Christians

Ask God to show you who might need this encouragement – newer Christians, long-time members of your church, or others.

Arrange to meet, then share with them why your regular time with God is so important to you. Suggest you start by meeting regularly, as sharing in common devotions is a beneficial way to learn how to develop an individual devotional life. In the beginning you might choose to meet 2-3 times a week, then less frequently as together you develop skills and confidence. What has helped me most to continue to be disciplined about growing spiritually all my life? Looking back I can see the link between the personal encouragement I received from others and my use of a printed resource such as one of Scripture Union's daily Bible reading booklets.

Depending on who you meet with, remember that your teaching may need to start right at the beginning.

Not all Christians are biblically literate and many have had little 'hands on' experience of finding their way around the Bible. So put your friends at ease so they are not self-conscious about their lack of basic knowledge – some may not know where to find the different books in the Bible or how to find chapter and verse. Others may lack confidence when pronouncing unfamiliar words. To help introduce them to a regular personal encounter with God, look for a step-by-step approach (see Chapter 2) and other key ideas found elsewhere in this handbook.

Non-literate people

Just because a person finds reading difficult does not mean they do not want to meet with God and respond to him. For some, a cassette of Bible readings is useful, but for most, a partner arrangement like the one described above, will be even more helpful.

As previously denied access to the written word becomes available, a partner can become a valued friend. Non-readers have often developed a retentive memory – once the words are heard, they are just as capable as those who can read when it comes to understanding and responding to the word. Others will need help in understanding what the passage is saying so they can work out how it might relate to them. Like all of us, they will appreciate encouragement to persevere when progress is slow or tough.

RECEIVE HELP FROM OTHERS

The Holy Spirit often uses other Christians as part of his work within you as an individual. It is good practice to consciously develop Christian friendships and know that the Holy Spirit will teach and guide you through them. Ask God to create opportunities for you to meet people who will encourage you, answer your questions, provide other viewpoints, show you new skills, and help you develop a wider whole-of-life perspective.

Some Christians benefit from a close friendship with a mature Christian person who allows them to discuss openly their spiritual 'ups and downs'. Being an 'older' Christian, they can share some of the joys that await you, and also point out various pitfalls that may confront you. Remember though that they are in no way superior to you but they can provide valuable guidance and direction, and model appropriate attitudes, values and lifestyles for younger disciples of Jesus Christ. As well, their feedback and advice will enhance your growth in intimacy with God, and they will learn things from you!

Ask God to show you a suitable person. Because sharing may become especially personal, it is preferable that the person is of the same sex as you.

INTEGRATE YOUR PERSONAL AND SMALL GROUP LIFE

Small groups provide the basic 'building blocks' for developing your individual Christian lifestyle and the part you play in the corporate lifestyle of your worshipping community.

Earlier in this chapter we noted ways you can enhance your personal spiritual growth when you meet with other Christians. Think about what opportunities already exist or which you can create, to integrate your personal times with God with regular meetings with a small group of fellow-Christians for Bible study, prayer, sharing and mission.

❋ Use your times together to demonstrate methods and skills which group members can use in their personal times with God. Many of the simple methods described in this book can be easily adapted for group settings, such as the 'Seven steps with God' method on page 159.

❋ Provide opportunities for members to share ideas and skills they have found helpful in their personal times with God. Make sure there is enough time allowed for members, especially the more reticent ones, to raise problems they face – other members may be able to help them resolve these. Be open to learning from one another.

* Put effort into making group times of prayer rich and fresh experiences. Guard against dullness, repetition and monotonous methods. Prayer is a learned skill, so introduce methods that can easily be adapted by members for their personal prayer times. For example, encourage *conversational prayer*, with members participating as a group in conversation with God:

  • Keep contributions short, with members praying often and in any order, each person consciously building on the previous person's prayer.

  • Incorporate silence before God as an ingredient of prayer.

  • Discourage the group from spending all its prayer time loading God with requests.

  • Remember to spend time praising and enjoying him too!

A handbook on praying in small groups, *Praying Together*[12], is a useful resource to encourage your creativity in this area.

If individual members of the group are able to read Bible passages in their personal regular encounters with God relating to what is studied in the small group meeting, there is a special bonus:

* Members don't have to do extra 'homework' during the week to prepare for their group time.

* *All* group members – not just the more vocal ones –

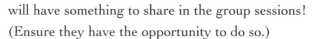

will have something to share in the group sessions!
(Ensure they have the opportunity to do so.)

❃ It will provide additional encouragement for members
to persevere in their personal times with God.

Integration such as this may need planning. Look out
for resource material such as Scripture Union's *Daily
Bread* – and use it in at least several 'blocks' of a few
weeks each year to provide continuity between
members' personal times with God and the group's
regular meeting time.

INTEGRATING PERSONAL SPIRITUAL GROWTH AND CORPORATE WORSHIP

Trying to integrate a person's spiritual formation with
other aspects of church life such as worship services
will demonstrate that encountering God, especially in
the Bible, is central to the life of your fellowship in
both attitude and action.

What can worship leaders do to enhance this
integration?

❃ *Encourage people to prepare for corporate worship.*
Suggest they read a Bible passage with a worship
orientation before they arrive. Give notice of the
passage (for example a Psalm) a week in advance
and incorporate the reading into your worship.

* *Give people opportunities to share how God is working in their lives.* Have them demonstrate how their regular times with God have equipped them for effective Christian living. Do this in small *ad hoc* groups or in a more planned way. This will depend on the size and dynamics of your congregation. Perhaps this could be made a regular feature of your corporate worship, followed by prayers of praise and intercession.

* *When choosing preaching topics for the year, build in several blocks of Sundays for topics based on daily Bible reading resources.* Encourage people to use these resources for their times with God, e.g. Scripture Union's quarterly booklets. The preaching will reinforce what they are reading privately and encourage them to persevere with their regular times with God. It will also motivate other members of the congregation to develop the discipline of a regular devotional time.

* *Structure sermons in the form of a simple Bible reading method and meditation.* The SU four-step method is quite suitable for this. Have the speaker start with some personal insights, then use an overhead projector or blackboard to record the people's discoveries and/or encourage people to share with others near them. Provide opportunities for people to pray for and with each other.

FAMILIES

One special support group where people can grow in their faith together is the *family unit*. Family dynamics give households the potential to be strategic incubators for the spiritual formation of members, children and adults alike. Meeting together with God can be a shared adventure for all family members, carried out at levels appropriate to their stage of development and leading to significant spiritual growth.

Busyness and lack of time are common excuses for why little of this happens in many households. If approached realistically, this situation need not continue. Four areas where spiritual growth can be encouraged within families are:

'Family worship'

'Family worship' (or 'family prayers') is a foreign idea to many families today. Some parents have reacted negatively to the concept because of childhood experiences. They recall being forced to sit through tedious sessions around the meal table. Others may resist trying again when their first efforts of family worship this failed. They remember their sense of frustration as they tried to cope with restless or uncooperative offspring. Or, as often is the case in my family, the sheer routines and pressures of life mean these times become shelved unintentionally and become hard to restart.

'Family worship' can be a time for encouraging a sense of family solidarity in the Christian faith. The key ingredients are similar to those used for your personal regular time with God:

❋ Be conscious of being in God's presence as a family;

❋ Have some input from the Bible;

❋ Explore what God is saying to the family members through the passage;

❋ Respond to God in prayer and follow this up with appropriate action.

Attitudes are important. It is essential for parents to be positive and relaxed – a sense of humour helps greatly. If some practices create resentment or boredom among family members, adults as well as the children, stop these and try something else!

Variety and *flexibility* are keys to making these times effective. There is no magic recipe that will cater for all families – what works will vary from family to family. How your family does it will depend on how your family expresses its life together. The age range of the children, the various reading abilities of family members and their interests, all need to be taken into account.

❋ *Be creative.* Experiment with newsprint, felt-pens, dressing up, play dough, spontaneous acting, music, dance, pictures, games. Make sure that the activity enables every family member to be involved and to learn by doing. Children and parents can contribute ideas for these times, and take responsibility for different aspects, all part of developing a genuine 'family' time, as well as encouraging initiative and leadership skills. For example, now that my sons are teenagers, each family member takes responsibility in turn for the format of our weekly family time. Resource books are available (see Appendix 3), but ideas will need to be adapted to your unique situation.

※ *Where and when?* All families are busy, but most can find some time to spend creatively with God. Use the natural gathering times of mealtime and bedtime, finding a time when family members are likely to be relaxed. Keep it informal, such as around a table or on the living room floor. You may aim for daily family worship but many families find they can comfortably achieve two to four sessions of five to fifteen minutes each week. Currently for my family, early Sunday evening is an opportunity to talk and pray about the activities of the coming week. Several years ago, Monday breakfast was the preferred time.

※ *Encourage a sense of worship.* Children have a great capacity for admiration and uninhibited worship and this can be a good example for adults. Accept the spontaneous ways your children choose to express their relationship with God, even if it is not quite the way you would go about it.

❋ *Be open to learning from each other.* If family members are open to learning from one another, each will benefit from the insights received. This will aid their spiritual development and bring them closer to God – parents can learn from their children, children from their siblings. Encourage this open attitude to create positive dynamics in your family life.

❋ *Be particularly sensitive.* Where one parent is not a committed Christian or unenthusiastic about the concept of family worship times, potential exists for tension and misunderstandings. If you are the enthusiastic one, share your vision with your partner, listening carefully to the response. If one partner decides not to participate, be sensitive to what is said concerning him/her when other family members have their devotional times.

Encourage your children in their own times with God

As your own regular encounter with God becomes important to you, share this with your children. Teach them how to listen to God, in keeping with their stage of development, and encourage their growing relationship with him.

✻ It is vastly more important to develop positive *attitudes* in the children towards God and the Bible than to maintain a strict daily devotional time. Be flexible, as the interest and enthusiasm of the children may fluctuate from week to week.

✻ Help your children find a few minutes in their day when they are quiet, relaxed and not readily distracted. Focus on the value of the time, not its length.

✻ Many resources are available to help children develop their own time with God. Look at Scripture Union's popular range of age-related Bible reading booklets (see Appendix 2). Work through the material with them at least occasionally, depending on their age and stage of development. Ask questions, help them with puzzles or answers, and encourage them to put ideas into their own words. Use a modern translation of the Bible such as the *Contemporary English Version* or the *Good News Bible* to assist their comprehension.

✻ Praise your children's efforts.

Couples together

A special 'spiritual partnership' can develop between partners when both are committed to growing in Christian discipleship. But it needs to be worked at – like many things in marriage, it will not happen instantly. And just because both partners are growing Christians, do not assume they are making headway in their praying and sharing together times.

Talk over the idea

Share together your expectations, fears and practical details. Each partner will have different ideas about how to structure this time together. For example, one may like to dig into the background of a Bible passage while the other may prefer to choose a verse or phrase to mull over. Or one may pray in a conversational style, with the other more comfortable praying aloud more formally.

Plan

Decide together what you will try to do:

* How will you incorporate the Bible into your time together with God? Will you read a section of the Bible and then pray about it? Will you discuss the section?
* Will you use a Bible reading guide? If so, which one?
* Will you pray silently or aloud? Will one pray for both, will you take it in turns, will you pray conversationally?
* Fix the time and place. This may sound obvious, but it is a key. Take into account your daily routines – but to give this time priority you may need to look at aspects of your lifestyle.

* What other features will you want to incorporate into this time? Will you experiment with music? Silence? Written prayers?

Be flexible

The *quality* of your time together is what counts, not maintaining a rigid but arid habit. There will be times when you cannot easily manage what is desirable, for example if you have a new baby, or a sick child. Accept your limitations – and don't set targets that you will find impossible to meet.

Some couples find that they can pray together only briefly on a daily basis – either first thing in the morning or last thing at night. They may need to plan for an extended time together with God once or twice a week. Others will experiment, finding different ways to express their life with God.

As your circumstances change and you find your plans do not work for some reason or other, be creative and look for other ways to develop your spiritual life together. For example, you may find you can take extra time at weekends or plan a monthly review to check on how your times with God are going. Holidays may also provide opportunities for doing some evaluation together.

Give each other space

Remember that partners need time alone with God as well as together. Do all you can to make it possible for your partner to have a personal time with God each day. For example, a husband can take responsibility for the children while his wife has a chance to meet with God.

Look for informal family opportunities for spiritual growth

Youth consultant Bruce Mullan believes that 'people are more likely to learn Christian faith in the same way as they learn their first language, not so much in a formal educational setting, as in a family environment and with adequate parent attention.' [13] Many church leaders echo these sentiments.

Members of a family interact with each other in a variety of informal, life-related settings and these can be used to enhance the growth of all the members. Whether these situations are in the home (a child's bedtime is often a natural setting) or 'out and about', they can provide a number of benefits:

▪ Life-settings can be used to highlight insights gained in their more formal times with God, resulting in a greater sense of spiritual integration. For example, if a family has been thinking about ways of caring for God's creation in their special 'family times with God', if they

see litter lying around when they visit the local
playground, they could put their insights into
practice and do some cleaning up.

* Real life issues often cause family members to
question what is happening. Use these as a stimulus
for going back to God with specific concerns and
issues. For example, witnessing a fight in a public
place between two adults may lead to questions at
home about anger, relationships, and care. This
would give a family the chance to look into the
Bible for insights, then to pray about aspects of the
concerns members have. Watching TV or videos
provides similar opportunities.

* Life situations give us opportunities to be mutually
accountable for our spiritual integrity. When a
parent driver exceeds the speed limit and their
young passenger comments, this should present the
driver with a challenge to reflect on the underlying
issue behind the comment.

* When a family member takes up a new activity,
fresh opportunities, attitudes and behaviours may
emerge, creating an expanded vision for the rest of
the family. And, when children entice adults to play,
their spontaneity can bring joy and free up the
adults inside. Reflection on this later may bring out
matters relating to the adult's relationship with

Christ. Or, when a child is allowed to participate in an 'adult-activity', such as playing a part in a church service or visiting people in some sort of need, a greater commitment to the church and to service may result.

To make appropriate connections between life-situations and Christian growth, special sensitivity is needed – especially by adults. It is far too easy to move from constructive insights to moralising (or preaching), manipulating, and/or destructive criticism. It is often difficult for adults to be open to learning from children. When the sense of mutuality and openness to one another is developed, the potential for ongoing spiritual growth is significant.

The family is an important social unit for spiritual development, and in these pages we have outlined various ways to enhance such development. I wish you well as you take some of these ideas, adapt them, and share the adventure of meeting God together in your family and household units!

Hazelnuts

TRY THESE
METHODS

'Do something
unusual. Be an
experimenter ... try
new experiences...
Poke some holes in
your rigidity. This
is not a time to be
timid. Take a
chance, it's worth it.'

TIM HANSEL

How long is it since you took the time to look around you to see the variety of God's creation? There are so many different flowers, insects, animals – even people! All reflect the wonderful creativity of God, a gift all who live in his world are able to enjoy.

Let God's creativity be reflected in your times with him day by day. You may have developed favourite methods of Bible reading and prayer, but you too can benefit from trying different approaches. Doing something different gives scope for seeing things from a fresh perspective. To help you to do that, some creative ways of approaching your time with God are outlined here.

Variety alone will not bring freshness to your relationship with God. To continue to achieve that means keeping in step with God and allowing his Spirit to control your life. Nevertheless, different methods can help get your thinking, reflecting and responding processes moving when you are seeking new and challenging directions under God.

KAIROS METHOD

Kairos is one of two Greek words the New Testament (originally written in the Greek language) uses for 'time'. It means 'time of opportunity and fulfilment' – an apt name for a method aimed at helping you in your special time with God!

When you have completed the 'prepare' and 'read' steps of your time with God, move into the 'explore' step in this way:

❋ Summarise the passage you have read in a few words.

❋ Think:

    • 'Is there a *God-thought* – something in the passage about God the Father, Jesus his son, and/or the Holy Spirit?'

    • 'Is there a *life-thought* – a command, promise, warning, good example or lesson – that stands out for me in the passage?'

    • 'Is there a *self-thought* for me today? What does God want me to do as a result of meeting him?' It may be a prayer, an action to take, or a discovery you have made.

❋ If a verse stands out for you from the passage you have read, write it down or memorise it.

❋ Move into the 'respond' phase of your time with God, drawing on the insights you have gained.

Example:

Matthew 6:31-34   8th June

SUMMARY:

As Christians serve God, they do not need to worry
about their basic needs, because God the Creator
understands their situation.

GOD-THOUGHT:

God my heavenly Father <u>knows</u> what I need (verse 31)
and is able to <u>provide</u> for those needs (verse 33).

LIFE-THOUGHT:

Verse 33: a <u>promise</u> with a condition: As disciples
focus on going God's way, he will provide for their
needs.

SELF-THOUGHT:

Priorities challenged today! Too concerned about
getting my bonus at work - and so not having the
energy to encourage John and Li Mun in their
discipleship. Arrange to see them this week.

SPECIAL VERSE:

Verse 33: 'But more than anything else, put God's
work first and do what he wants. Then the other
things will be yours as well.'

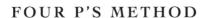

FOUR P'S METHOD

As with the Kairos method, use this especially for the 'explore' phase of your time with God.

❋ **Pretend** to be the editor of a newspaper – provide a 4-6 word summary headline for the section you have read.

❋ **Parallel:** what other Bible passages bring out the same idea as this one? What do they add to your understanding of the theme of the passage – or its key words and thoughts? Use the footnotes and cross-references printed in many Bibles and a Bible concordance (see Appendix 2) to help you find appropriate passages.

❋ **Problem:** is there something you do not understand, or find difficult to accept? If you cannot resolve this at the time, note down the problem and ask a Christian friend later or look up a resource book for an answer.

❋ **Profit:** is there a specific thing you need to do to profit from this passage?

Example:

PASSAGE: Romans 8:31-39

HEADLINE: 'Christians inseparable from God's love'

PARALLEL:

* Romans 5:8: how much God loves us.

* Psalm 139:7-12: highlights that there is no place anywhere where God can not be.

* 1 John 2:1-2: even my sin need not keep God away from me.

PROBLEM: How can a Christian (and that's me!) have the same sense of certainty that Paul has (verse 38)?

PROFIT:

* I need to keep verses 38-39 ('nothing can separate us from his love...') in mind when Phil and Sarah try to undermine my faith with those hard questions.

* Goal: memorise verses 38-39 by Thursday.

AEIOU METHOD

After you have read the selected section of the Bible, follow this sequence to help you think and reflect:

* *Ask* questions about what you have read:
    * who?   * what?   * where?
    * when?   * why?   * how?

* **Emphasise** the important words (i.e. words of action, name or description). Read key parts of the passage aloud several times, stressing different words each time. Analyse the words. What do they mean? Do they have different shades of meaning?

* **In your own words** try to restate the passage. You can do this in a number of creative ways, e.g.
  * Paraphrase it (rewrite it your own way);
  * Write a poem, psalm, song or prayer that reflects the content of the passage;
  * Draw a picture or create a poster (God loves colour!).

* **Other references.** Compare the section you are reading with related parts of the Bible. The footnotes and cross-references in your Bible and a Bible concordance will help you find these. What do they add to your understanding of the passage? Do they provide a balance or a contrast?

* **Use.** What will you apply in your life as a result of your thoughts on the passage? How will you do it? When will you do it? What practical results might occur?

LIVING AND PRAYING THE BIBLE

To appreciate the significance of a Bible passage, use your imagination and enter the passage as if you are a participant. The Gospels and Acts lend themselves particularly well to this method, as do the straightforward storytelling (narrative) passages found in the Old Testament.

* Make sure your posture is one you find conducive to spending time with God.
* Pick a short passage and read it slowly.
* Imagine you are present at the event described in the passage. Use your imagination to experience the sights, sounds and feelings described or suggested by the event.
  * Assume the role of one of the characters or an observer. Try to appreciate what is happening from the perspective of that person.
  * Apply your five senses to the situation. What might you see? Hear? Smell? Touch? Taste?
  * Reflect on how you feel or react as a participant in the event.
* Don't rush. When you find a natural 'resting place' in the passage, take time to pause. Savour the encounter.
* Share your thoughts with God.

Example:

Read the account of Jesus healing a paralysed man in Mark 2:1-12. Imagine that *you are the paralysed man*. What are some of the questions or emotions running through your mind?

* How do you feel about your four friends and their faith?

* What is it like being lowered through the roof of the house down onto the floor in front of Jesus?
* What is the atmosphere in the room with so many people crowding in – stuffy and smelly?
* Imagine looking up from the floor into the faces of so many people, including Jesus.
* What do you think and feel when Jesus says to you, 'My son, your sins are forgiven'? How do you think he says it?
* What do you think and feel as Jesus speaks to the teachers of the Law?
* What goes on inside you when Jesus tells you to 'Get up, pick up your mat, and go home!'?

You could also put yourself in the place of one of the other characters, for example, one of the four friends of the paralysed man; a teacher of the Law; someone outside the house trying to see what is going on; even the owner of the house (who is going to pay to repair your roof?!).

Use these insights as a participant 'back then', to stimulate thinking about your relationship with God and others in your life, and your faith today.

'Praying the Gospels'

The four Gospels – each in their own distinctive way – portray an understanding of who Jesus is and how he challenges people from a wide variety of backgrounds and situations to consider the quality of their commitment to God's ways. They are an especially rich source for helping us to develop *our* faith and ability to pray.

The 'Living and praying the Bible' method is especially good for developing an ability to open up the whole of our lives to be formed by God – often termed *contemplation*. It can be used with the Gospel passages where Jesus encounters people. The ability to contemplate is not something we conjure up for ourselves but comes to us much like a gift.

How can you become more contemplative? Focus on Jesus as portrayed in a passage from one of the Gospels, using the guidelines suggested in the 'Living and praying the Bible' method above. Allow yourself to be drawn into his presence:

* *Be there* with him, recognising that just as Jesus met persons in the Gospel event in their unique circumstances, so he can meet you in your particular circumstances.
* *Want* him to be there, as you would eagerly want someone special to spend good quality time with you.
* *Listen* to him. Listen with trust and faith. Listen with gratitude for what he offers you.
* *Let* him ... let him be with you. Let him be to you what he wants to be. Let him speak to you. Let him forgive

you, strengthen you, challenge you. Allow him to
do what he knows is best for you at this time.

* *Respond* to him. Do this in the way you think is best,
rather than in ways you think you *ought* to respond.
Be yourself. Depending on the occasion, these may
be words of praise or gratitude or other feelings
expressed at the time (even those of disappointment
or anger). Or, you may choose to quietly experience
the calmness of Jesus' presence.[14]

Appreciate these times of real closeness to God, Jesus,
and the Holy Spirit. Many Christians find they do not
come often but when they do, they can be profoundly
life-moulding and memorable.

'Praying the Psalms'

On page 92 we referred to the use of the psalms in
prayer.

The book of Psalms is the world's most famous
prayer journal. In effect it is the Bible's own handbook
on how to express yourself to God in praise and in
prayer. These 150 psalms give us a glimpse into the
soul of the Israelites, providing some of the most
profound expressions ever written of people's thoughts
and feelings in relation to God. All of life's experiences
can be found there, times of joy, deep doubt,
depression, anger, and thankfulness.

To Athanasius, a Christian leader of the fourth century, this collection of sacred songs occupied a unique place in the Bible. He noted that while most of the Scriptures speak to people (i.e. words from God to us), the Psalms speak *for* people (i.e. words spoken to God or about God) about the realities of life.

The Psalms speak for us just as they did for the Israelites. We experience the same common range of emotions as we face various life situations and react similarly. Using psalms in our times with God can be helpful in two main ways:

* They can help us be honest in expressing our own deep feelings about life and about God. Whenever we hear the psalm-writer's reaction to life, and find ourselves responding, 'Hey, that's the way I sometimes feel. Is it OK to feel that way?', we are being honest with God.

* They cause us to consider God's ways, their colourful imagery capturing our imagination and inviting us to discover truth about God.

When we use psalms in these ways, they can *stimulate, express,* and *deepen* our relationship with God. By learning the way in which the psalm-writers expressed themselves to God, we too can learn to express ourselves to God.

How then can you proceed in 'Praying the Psalms'? You could try to use them in some of the following ways:

✻ Use the guidelines above for putting yourself into a passage of Scripture, especially the five attitudes for contemplation (in 'Praying the Gospels' on p. 147). However, instead of imagining yourself in an event, allow yourself to experience the images and feelings described in the psalm.

As you read the psalm slowly – either silently or aloud – as soon as some part attracts your attention pause. Why have you noted it? Does it express your experience? Does it grate on you? Does it remind you of a particular situation or relationship? Does it draw out particular emotions in you? Share your responses with God.

✻ The Israelites sang the psalms – so can we! Perhaps you already know a tune for the psalm you are reading, for example such well-known hymns as 'All people that on earth do dwell' (Psalm 100) or 'The king of love, my shepherd is' (Psalm 23). Alternatively, you could compose your own tune.

✻ The Israelites refer often to key past events in their history, ones in which they were especially aware of God's presence, protection and care. Rewrite a psalm, incorporating your own life-experiences to reflect the same mood and feeling. What are the special events in your pilgrimage with God? Use your 'personalised psalm' as a stimulus to prayer.

❋ As part of your preparation to meet with God, develop a habit of reading through the psalms regularly – perhaps one each day. Christian editor John Lane, suggests that when we do this, 'we will be touched by a wide range of emotions and responses. Some days the psalm's mood will match our own. We will have the vocabulary we need. At other times the psalm will be 'up' when we are feeling 'down', or dark when we are feeling alive. These contrasts will also help us to identify with the needs of others around us and with the traumas of the world.'

'MARK MY WORD' METHOD

'Mark my word' provides a framework for reflecting on a Bible passage. It uses arrows marked beside the Bible text, leading into a prayer response to what God is communicating to you in the passage.

❋ Read the passage and as you read, draw small arrows in the margin of your Bible according to the discoveries you make, based on the middle column ('For discoveries about...') of the key on next page.

❋ After marking in the arrows, respond in prayer, using as a guide for your prayer the words suggested in the third column ('Key words for your prayer response') of the key as guides.

'Mark my word' key

Direction of arrow	For discoveries about...	Key words for your prayer response
↑	God... the Father Jesus his Son the Holy Spirit	• *Praise* God for who he is and for the things I have discovered about him in the passage. • *Thank* God for what the passage reminds me he has done for me: for helping... healing... leading... correcting.
↓	Us: the sort of people we are without God, and the problems we meet when in conflict with him	• *Forgive* me for my failures. • *Strengthen* me to overcome the temptations read about. • *Protect* me from the sins described. • *Rescue* me when I am reminded of a sin not easy to overcome.
→	Directions for living with God	• *Help* me to put into practice what I have learnt. • *Lead* me in new directions pointed out. • *Teach* me about what I don't understand. • *Keep* me faithfully following as God continues to lead.

* *Either* respond in prayer to each arrow as you mark it in the passage or if you prefer, mark arrows through the whole passage. Then go back and pray about each one individually or all the ideas you found relating to a particular area of discovery.

* Don't force yourself to find examples of all three arrow directions in a passage. You may find places for only one or two of the arrow directions. On rare occasions, for example in some Old Testament passages, you may not be able to find material for any arrow.

NOTE: The arrows in your Bible provide a permanent reminder about your discoveries. However, if you do not want to mark your Bible, use inexpensive copies of single Bible books, available from Christian bookshops. Other alternatives are to photocopy the relevant pages or download the text you require from the Internet.

Example:

⟶ 'If you love me you will do as I command. Then I will

↑ ask the Father to send you the Holy Spirit who will help

you and always be with you. The Spirit will show you ↑

what is true.

The people of this world can't accept the Spirit, because ↓

↓ they don't see or know him. But you know the Spirit, ⟶

who is with you and will keep on living in you.' ⟶

(John 14:15-17)

154

Possible prayer responses from this passage:

1. 'Thank you God, that you've given us your Spirit to show us the truth.'

2. 'Please forgive me for the times when I've not recognised that you are present, especially among my family members.'

3. 'Just as you keep close to me, please help me constantly to build a deeper relationship with you.'

LIVING WITH A BIBLE BOOK

Once you have read through a number of books of the Bible as part of your times with God over a period of months (and years) you will have gained a valuable overview of God's written message to humanity. However, occasionally you may want to immerse yourself in one particular Bible book for an extended lengthy period, to explore it in detail. Such in-depth reading can lead to discoveries you may well miss in your less intensive daily reading.

* First choose your Bible book. You may want to live with one of the Gospels for a few months, to build up a comprehensive picture of Jesus. Or you might want to delve into one of Paul's letters, or an Old Testament prophetic book.

* Read the book through in one sitting for a broad overview of the direction and message of the book

(see 'Read individual books in one sitting' on p. 57). Make an outline of the book, based on its main sections or the development of its major theme(s).

❋ In your regular times with God, read the book section by section. Try to understand each section in its context, and ask God what he is communicating through it. This phase may take some weeks, as you explore the detail of the book. (You will probably need extra time to check out the meaning of words, to cross-reference to other parts of the Bible, and to look up resource books to answer your questions.)

❋ Meditate on your discoveries during the day. Recall some portion of your reading and relate its meaning to your present situation. Memorise key verses to help you recall key phrases and ideas.

❋ Use your discoveries as a basis for your prayers. Talk with God about the things you found important through your reading and reflection.

❋ As you proceed you may uncover various aspects of the book that you want to explore further. Note these, and take them up in subsequent readings of the book. For example, you may want a more detailed look at a particular person featured there, or follow up a theme or idea emphasised in the book.

❋ Keep a record of your observations, questions and answers. When you look back you will find that your knowledge of the book increases, and – more importantly – you will track your growing relationship with the author of the book. That's what the Bible is for!

KRINO

This method will challenge your approach to biblical reflection. It starts with you looking at your personal situation, then checking your response against what the Bible is saying in that situation. *Krino* is a Greek word meaning 'to judge, decide, determine' – and this method will enable you to judge your life with reference to the Bible. Its basis is that God is alive and working in his world. As you prayerfully look and listen, you will find that God uses events to draw you closer to him. Follow these steps:

* *Situation.* Ask 'In what recent events has God been speaking to me? When have I been challenged or aroused to thought or action?'

  Example: 'Person X at work is a pain in the neck. He is always putting me down and it's so irritating!'

* *Message.* Ask 'What is God telling me about himself, myself and others through the situation?'

  Example: 'I think God wants me to remember that X is as important to him as I am... X needs to know that God can help him deal with the underlying reasons for why he behaves like this. God is also challenging me to check my reactions to X whenever he makes his comments.'

❧ *Response.* Ask 'How do I normally respond? How could (or should) I respond in the light of what God is saying to me?'

Example: 'I usually react by snapping back at X; but I think Jesus would exercise patience and pray for him. That's what I should do too, and try to find opportunities to get to know him better and to talk to him about Jesus.'

❧ *Confirmation.* Ask 'What does the Bible say to me about this situation?' Ask the Holy Spirit to lead you to a principle or passage in the Bible that speaks to that particular situation. (A concordance or other Bible reference books will help you find appropriate references.)

Example: 'Jesus' teaching in the Sermon on the Mount about anger comes to mind (Matthew 5:21-22); also Matthew 18:21-35 about forgiving those who offend me. Do I need to look for a chance to talk about it with X? Matthew 18:15 seems to indicate I should!'

❧ *Test.* Ask 'Is my confirmation balanced?' Check your findings with a mature Christian, to ascertain that your discoveries fit in with the overall thrust of the Bible.

Example: (Several days later) 'I spoke with my home group leader. He thinks I need to pray and then go to X. He suggested that God might be saying something about my need for more patience and tolerance with people and pointed me to the principle in Ephesians 4:2 and Colossians 3:13. The home group members are going to pray with me.'

Krino is designed for people who are reasonably well acquainted with the Bible and its message. While able to be used by an individual, several people working together can also share insights about the situation, message and response. Together they can seek God's guidance in the Bible for the confirmation.

To get full benefit from the method, and to assure you that you are using the Bible with integrity, it is important to become aware of your filters (cultural, doctrinal, and personal – see pp. 74ff). You also need to develop your skills of how to apply biblical insights appropriately (see Chapter 5).

SEVEN STEPS WITH GOD

This method of Bible meditation originated in Africa and is especially good to use when meeting with a friend or friends. Where it is often helpful is in situations where participants differ in their levels of spiritual maturity.

1. Invite the Lord

One person invites God to be present. God is already there, but a conscious invitation helps you to focus on his presence, and be open to him.

2. *Read the text*
3. *Look at the text*

   Allow the message of the text to 'soak in'. What words, phrases or ideas strike you in a special way? If in a group, participants can read aloud the words or phrases that have impressed them. Don't discuss at this stage – listen, and allow a short time of silence after each contribution.

4. *Let God speak*

   Read the passage again. Have a time of silence. Be open to God.

5. *Share what has been heard*

   What insights or feelings do you have? Share these – but avoid preaching or debate.

6. *Search together*

   Ask 'what does the Lord want me/us to do?' Express your needs and hopes, and how the Bible passage meets or challenges them.

7. *Pray*

   Allow the words of the Bible to become 'food' for prayer.

You may wish to write out these section headings on a small bookmark as a reminder and have it in front of you whenever you use it.

ENDWORD

What are the secrets of Christian growth?

To answer this question, learning about the wide range of ideas and methods outlined in this handbook is only a start – but an *important* start. What you have to do next is to *apply* some of these suggestions. Then you can deepen your relationship with God grow more mature.

As you move forward, note these two counterbalancing comments:

DON'T BE DAUNTED

In any journey – for example travelling to another town or country, or running a marathon – what is important is to get started and keep moving forwards, even though the final destination seems far in the distance. In your life with God as a disciple of Jesus, you need to know that you are neither alone nor without resources. God understands your unique requirements for growing in your relationship with him, and provides all you need through the Holy Spirit 'walking alongside you'. It is your responsibility to recognise and use those resources!

THINK BIG!

This handbook provides ideas to help you develop your relationship with God in quite specific areas. As you progress, you will need more challenges to build on the foundations already laid in your life.

These lie in learning about other practices that are available to help you grow. Traditionally, these were called 'the disciplines of the Christian life'. Use them as part of your everyday living. Richard Foster, has written an excellent book, *Celebration of discipline*.[15] There he invites Christians to start to use these practices to allow 'the abundance of God into our lives'.

In this handbook we have focused on the disciplines of meditation, prayer and (to a lesser extent) study of the Bible. Foster suggests a wider range of practices. The ones he finds important are:

* *'Inward disciplines'* – meditation, prayer, fasting, and study.
* *'Outward disciplines'* – simplicity of lifestyle, solitude (times of being alone), submission to others, and service of others.
* *'Corporate disciplines'* (those which we do with other Christians) – confession, worship, seeking guidance, and joyous celebration.

Look for opportunities to discover more about these

practices, seeking to adopt them as part of your ongoing growth with God.

What, then, are the secrets of Christian growth? Like the trees referred to in the Introduction, it is essential to put down roots to the source of life-giving nourishment. The God-supplied source is available to each of us. Various means of putting down our roots have been outlined in the pages of this handbook. It is now over to you to put the two together – for your life, and for your growth. Go to it, with God!

APPENDIX 1:
The basis of the four-step pattern for times with God

The four-step pattern which is outlined in this handbook in Chapter 2 (p. 27) is one which Scripture Union has encouraged people to use for many years. Numerous Christians have attested to its helpfulness.

The Scripture Union pattern is not a recent innovation. Key features of the pattern have their roots to the Christian monasteries of the 12th century AD, where a method of prayerful reading of the Bible called *Lectio Divina* was developed. The method proved to be so effective that it became a central part of the life of a number of religious orders. While often considered to be a method 'owned' by Roman Catholics, a wide range of Christians increasingly uses it.

Lectio Divina (= 'divine reading'), as a means of reading the Bible to encourage a transforming encounter with God, has four steps:

❋ *Lectio* (= reading)

The process of reading the Bible text.

❋ *Meditatio* (= meditation)

Processing what has been received from the Bible text – the 'chewing' process (see p. 64) in which the text and our everyday lives inter-relate with each other.

❋ *Oratio* (= prayer)

Responding to God on the basis of what we have read and meditated upon.

❧ *Contemplatio* (= contemplation)

The sense of yielding to God for 'what he wants to do in us, with us, through us.'[16]

Practical ways in which each of these four steps can be developed have been outlined in the different chapters of this handbook. If you want to learn more about *Lectio Divina*, the Catholic Biblical Federation's bulletin, *Dei verbum* (English Edition) often carries articles on the subject. A good introductory article appears in No. 46 1/1998.

A new/old way of Praying the Bible

In the spirit of *Lectio Divina*, Pauline Hoggarth (Scripture Union's International Bible Ministries Consultant) invites us to "Pray the Bible" using the themes of the SU Method outlined on page 27:

❧ *Come to God*

Come to the Lord as you are. Worship him for his power, greatness and majesty. Bring him your feelings and needs. Ask for his Holy Spirit to help you to understand and respond to what you read.

❧ *Read* the Bible passage slowly and thoughtfully, listening out for what God is saying to you.

❧ *Talk with God* about what you have read. These suggestions may help you:

- Lord, thank you for your word to me today. What special message are you shouting out to me, or whispering to me, in these verses?

- Lord, I want to meet *you* here, show me more about yourself Father, Son or Holy Spirit in these verses.
- I don't know what today holds for me, Lord. I need your guidance, your advice. I need you to help me be alert. Direct my heart and thoughts to those words you know I need.
- Lord your word is a mirror in which I often find myself. Show me myself here, as you see me, alone or with others. Thank you that you understand how I feel as I read your word.
- Lord, there are things here I don't understand. Please help me through the SU Guide or give me others who may help me.

❋ *Respond*

If you have a copy of the SU Guide, read it now. Try to write down a word to carry with you which has come to you through this passage. Pray for others who are on your mind at the moment. Determine to share your experiences with others.

APPENDIX 2:
Resources for developing times with God

Naturally, a Bible is the *key* resource. Other printed resources are no substitute for the Bible itself, although they can provide valuable assistance.

DAILY BIBLE READING BOOKLETS

A wide variety of printed books and booklets are available to help you in your regular times with God.

Not all achieve the same goals. How can your select an appropriate one? The following questions may help you to make your choice:

* Do the daily comments encourage you to actually open and 'dig into' the Bible for yourself or merely tell you what the writer has discovered?

* Is a major part of the Bible covered over a period of time – to enable you to appreciate God's wider perspective?

* Do the printed comments in the booklet help you to develop skills to enable you to use the Bible more effectively?

* Do the printed comments challenge you to examine your behaviour and attitudes or merely reinforce your current position?

❋ Can the booklets be integrated into small groups and/or church worship?

Quarterly booklets of daily Bible readings with comments, available from Scripture Union, often meet most of these criteria. The current range includes:

❋ **Dated booklets**

Closer to God (has a lively approach to Bible themes and books)

Daily Bread (covers most of the Bible, helping you to ask 'What is the Bible saying to me today?')

Encounter with God (for in-depth study, with introductory notes and cross-references)

One Up (for 11-14 year olds)

Hotshots (for 8-9 year olds)

Snapshots (for 9-10 year olds)

❋ **Undated books of Bible readings with comments, from Scripture Union**

The *Foothold* series (Three books giving an introduction to the Bible in 100 short readings, so becoming a 300 part course)

DAYZD (for older teenagers. Six books with a quarter's readings)

Some of these resources are available on the Internet: http://www.scripture.org.uk

❋ **Other publications which guide you through the Bible**

Dennis Lennon, *Through the Bible in a year – A spiritual journal* (Scripture Union, 1997)

John R. Kohlenberger III, *Read Through the Bible in a Year* (Moody Press, 1986). This booklet has a reading plan plus brief introductions to each book of the Bible.

The One Year Bible (Tyndale House, 1986) has 365 readings
    from the *New International Version* or *The Living Bible,* each
    with selections from the Old and New Testaments.
Several publishers have one year Bibles in different
translations of the Bible. Talk to the people at your
Christian bookshop for the one that will suit you.

BUILD UP YOUR OWN RESOURCE LIBRARY

'What does that word mean, I wonder?' 'Why is this issue
mentioned in the Bible passage?' 'Where is that place?'

As you read the Bible you will find yourself asking
questions like these. Even if you are using a daily Bible
reading booklet, the answers may not be immediately
available. It is helpful to acquire a small number of
resources to enable you to dig deeper into the Bible and help
answer some of your questions. Of course – as with daily
Bible reading booklets – they are no substitute for the Bible
itself.

What resources might be most useful?

❋ *Several versions of the Bible*, to see how they have rendered
    the original text of the Bible (in Hebrew and Greek
    mainly) into modern English. A good combination is
    either the readable *Good News Bible* or *Contemporary
    English Version*, alongside the more traditional *New
    International Version* or *New Revised Standard Version*. You
    might also appreciate a modern paraphrase of the Bible like

Eugene Peterson's *The Message*, for reading larger chunks or whole books of the Bible in one sitting.

❋ *A Bible commentary* or *handbook* outlines the main themes of the books of the Bible chapter by chapter. The content and meaning of the passages are emphasised. Difficulties and problem areas are treated in detail. *The Lion Handbook to the Bible* and *The New Bible Commentary* (InterVarsity Press) are recommended one-volume commentaries.

❋ *A Bible dictionary or encyclopedia* will give you the background to the people of the Bible, their customs, and the lands in which they lived. A knowledge of the situation of the original readers and hearers of the Scriptures will help you better understand what God is saying to us today. A good Bible dictionary – with its colourful maps, biographical sketches of Bible characters, illustrations and diagrams – is a valuable asset. Consider either *The Lion Encyclopedia of the Bible* or the *New Bible Dictionary* (InterVarsity Press).

❋ A concordance lists the words used in the Bible, and the places where those words are used. Some of its key uses are

- to help you locate verses when you can remember only one or two words from the verse.
- to help you discover more fully what words mean, seeing the different shades of meaning various Bible writers give to the words.

- to see how often a word is used in the Bible – and in what books it appears. A concordance may list not only English words used in the Bible, but also the words in the Hebrew and Greek languages of the original Bible manuscripts. This enables you to discover when the same word in English has been used for more than one Hebrew or Greek word (and vice versa).

Young's Concordance and Strong's Concordance (based on the Authorised Version of the Bible) have been popular for many years; and concordances are also available for most of the new Bible translations.

* *A Bible atlas,* such as the *New Bible Atlas* (IVP, Leicester, 1985) with its maps, charts and geographical information, can be an asset to help you get a feel for the 'reality' of Bible story enabling you to visualise actual events in real places.

Traditionally, the range of resources outlined above was available only in book form. Now, almost all can be obtained as computer software, or accessed through internet websites. Because the choice is so large and varied, ask for advice on what to select from your church leaders or local Christian bookshop.

The financial outlay on such resources may seem considerable but when you weigh up the cost against the use you will make of them over a period of years, they represent real value for money.

APPENDIX 3:
For further reading

The following books are useful tools to assist your growth. You can also ask Christian friends for advice on books they have found helpful.

USING AND INTERPRETING THE BIBLE

Gordon S. Dicker, *The Bible with Understanding* (Joint Board of Christian Education, Melbourne, 1988; revised edition 1996).

John Drane, *Introducing the Old Testament* (Lion Publishing, UK, 1987) and *Introducing the New Testament* (Lion Publishing, UK, 1986).

Gordon D. Fee and Douglas Stewart, *How to Read the Bible for all its Worth* (Scripture Union-UK, 1981; reprinted 1993).

Euan Fry, *Which Bible Translation for Me?* (Bible Society in Australia, 1985).

Jack Kuhatschek, *Taking the Guesswork out of Applying the Bible* (Inter-Varsity Press, Leicester, 1991).

John Stott, *Understanding the Bible* (Scripture Union-UK, reissued 1997).

Christopher Wright, *User's Guide to the Bible* (Lion, 1984; hard back 1995).

PRAYER

Joyce Huggett, *Listening to God* (Hodder and Stoughton, 1986; revised 1996).

Bill Hybels, *Too Busy not to Pray* (IVP, USA, revised edition 1997).

Roy Lawrence, *How to Pray when Life Hurts* (IVP, USA, 1993, Scripture Union-UK, 1997).

Eugene Peterson, *Answering God: The Psalms as tools for prayer* (Harper, San Francisco, 1989).

Alfred Stanway, *Prayer* (Acorn Press, Melbourne, 1991).

GROWING IN SPIRITUAL DISCIPLINES

Richard Foster, *Celebration of Discipline* (Hodder and Stoughton, revised 1998).

Brother Lawrence, *The Practice of the Presence of God* (Hodder, new edition 1997 with study guide).

Gordon McDonald, *Ordering Your Private World* (Highland Books, UK, 1988).

M. Robert Mulholland Jr., *Invitation to a journey: A road map for spiritual formation* (IVP, USA, 1993). (Contains chapters on personality and spiritual growth.)

J.I. Packer, *Knowing God* (Hodder and Stoughton, 1994, 2nd edition).

John White, *The Fight* (IVP, USA, 1977).

SPIRITUALITY AND PERSONALITY

B. Duncan, *Pray Your Way: Your personality and God* (Dartman, Longman & Todd, 1994).

Leslie J. Francis, *Personality Type and Scripture: Exploring Mark's Gospel* (Mowbray, 1997).

Martin Goldsmith, *Knowing Me, Knowing God* (SPCK, 1994).

BROADEN YOUR VIEW OF THE SCOPE OF THE BIBLE

John Stott, *Issues Facing Christians Today* (Marshall, Morgan and Scott, 1984; 3rd edition, Harper Collins, 1999).

GUIDANCE

P. Jensen & A. Payne, *Guidance & the Voice of God* (Matthias Media, Sydney, 1997).

Janet Lumb, *Guidance* (Scripture Union-UK, 1985).

Charles W. Shepson, *How to Know God's Will* (Christian Publications, 1998).

G.T. Smith, *Listening to God in Times of Choice* (IVP, USA, 1997).

JOURNAL WRITING

Edward England, Ed., *Keeping a Spiritual Journal* (Highland Books, UK, 1988, out of print).

Richard Peace, *Spiritual Journalling: Recording your journey toward God* (Navpress, CO, 1995).

SMALL GROUPS

Allan Harkness, *Praying Together: A handbook to encourage more effective prayer in small groups* (Scripture Union Australia 1996).

John Mallison, *The Small Group Leader* (Openbook Publishers, Adelaide, 1996).

FAMILIES

Family Glue, John & Judith Simpson (Scripture Union Australia, 1997).

Find Out series (Scripture Union Australia) – especially designed for parents to use with 5–7's.

Jigsaw series (Scripture Union-UK) – introducing 3–5's to the Bible.

Merry Go Round the Bible (Scripture Union) – 30 simple three minute devotions for families.

ENDNOTES:

1 John Laird, *No Mere Chance,* Hodder & Stoughton and Scripture Union, London, 1981, p. 19.

2 *Knowing God,* Hodder and Stoughton, London, 1973.

3 'Spiritual Reading of Scripture', in Weavings, Vol. III, No. 6, November/December 1988, p. 30.

4 Laird, p. 62.

5 Richard Foster, *Celebration of Discipline*, Hodder & Stoughton, London, 1978, p. 30.

6 Laird, p. 45.

7 Laird, p. 58.

8 Sheila Pritchard, 'Spiritual Growth, Spiritual Hunger', *Reaper*, December 1989-January 1990, p. 5.

9 Adapted from B. V. Hill, *The Greening of Christian Education*, Lancer Books, NSW, 1985, pp. 110-112.

10 Laird, p. 62.

11 Brother Lawrence, *The Practice of the Presence of God*, Mowbrays, London, 1980, p. 15.

12 Allan Harkness, *Praying Together: A handbook to encourage more effective prayer in small groups*, Scripture Union Australia, 1996.

13 Bruce Mullan, What Can We Learn at School? *Australian Ministry Digest*, 1995, Vol. 2, No. 3, pp. 2-4.

14 These five areas have been drawn from a photocopy of a short article, *Praying the Gospels*, by Armand Nigro. The source of the article is not known.

15 Richard Foster, *Celebration of Discipline: The path to spiritual growth*, London, Hodder & Stoughton, London, 1990.

16 M. Robert Mulholland Jr, *Invitation to a Journey: A road map for spiritual formation*, IVP, USA, 1993, p. 114.